The Changing South

*Trans-*action Books

The Changing South

Edited by
RAYMOND W. MACK

Trans-action Books

Published and distributed by
Aldine Publishing Company

The essays in this book originally appeared
in *Trans-action* Magazine

TA Book-3
Library of Congress Catalog Number: 75-91126

Contents

Preface

However diverse their attitudes and interpretations may sometimes be, social scientists are now entering a period of shared realization that the United States—both at home and abroad—has entered a crucial period of transition. Indeed, the much burdened word "crisis" has now become a commonplace among black militants, Wall Street lawyers, housewives, and even professional politicians.

For the past six years, *Trans*-action magazine has dedicated itself to the task of reporting the strains and conflicts within the American system. But the magazine has done more than this. It has pioneered in social programs for changing the society, offered the kind of analysis that has permanently restructured the terms of the "dialogue" between peoples and publics, and offered the sort of prognosis that makes for real alterations in social and political policies directly affecting our lives.

The work done in the pages of *Trans*-action has crossed

disciplinary boundaries. This represents much more than simple cross-disciplinary "team efforts." It embodies rather a recognition that the social world cannot be easily carved into neat academic disciplines. That, indeed, the study of the experience of blacks in American ghettos, or the manifold uses and abuses of agencies of law enforcement, or the sorts of overseas policies that lead to the celebration of some dictatorships and the condemnation of others, can best be examined from many viewpoints and from the vantage points of many disciplines.

This series of books clearly demonstrates the superiority of starting with real world problems and searching out practical solutions, over the zealous guardianship of professional boundaries. Indeed, it is precisely this approach that has elicited enthusiastic support from leading American social scientists for this new and dynamic series of books.

The demands upon scholarship and scientific judgment are particularly stringent, for no one has been untouched by the current situation. Each essay republished in these volumes bears the imprint of the author's attempt to communicate his own experience of the crisis. Yet, despite the sense of urgency these papers exhibit, the editors feel that many have withstood the test of time, and match in durable interest the best of available social science literature. This collection of *Trans*-action articles, then, attempts to address itself to immediate issues without violating the basic insights derived from the classical literature in the various fields of social science.

The subject matter of these books concerns social changes that have aroused the long-standing needs and present-day anxieties of us all. These changes are in organizational life styles, concepts of human ability and intelligence, changing patterns of norms and morals, the relationship of social conditions to physical and biological environments, and in the status of social science with national policy making.

This has been a decade of dissident minorities, massive shifts in norms of social conduct, population explosions and urban expansions, and vast realignments between nations of the world. The social scientists involved as editors and authors of this *Trans*-action series have gone beyond observation of these critical areas, and have entered into the vital and difficult tasks of explanation and interpretation. They have defined issues in a way making solutions possible. They have provided answers as well as asked the right questions. Thus, this series should be conceived as the first collection dedicated not to the highlighting of social problems alone, but to establishing guidelines for social solutions based on the social sciences.

THE EDITORS
Trans-action

Introduction

RAYMOND W. MACK

This has been a century of drastic institutional change in America—change in quality of education, in quantity of education, in income distribution, in the extension of suffrage. The South has participated in these massive changes but it is still far behind every other region of the country.

The 1956 data used in my article on the white Southerner indicate that "ten states spent less than $200 per pupil on education, and every one of the ten was a Southern state," while "thirty-one states spent $250 or more per pupil and not one of them was in the South."

A decade after the 1954 Supreme Court decision on school desegregation, the amount of money invested per year in education had changed but the pattern of distribution had not. The annual per pupil commitment had risen to the point where the bottom nine states were spending more than $200 but less than $300 per pupil—and every one of those nine was a Southern state. The top twenty-seven states were spending over $400 per pupil and not one of those states was in the South.

The only census statistics where we expect to find Southern states competing for top positions are those that indicate social pathology such as illiteracy and malnutrition. The South has formed the base of the American social pyramid in most ways except the one dear to fanciers of the ante bellum myth. The notion of the Old South as a genteel cradle of American culture loses a good deal in the translation from myth to reality. Histories of the development of the American novel, painting, poetry, and music before 1860 can be written with scant reference to the contribution of the South. The truth is nearer H. L. Mencken's acid characterization of that region as the "Sahara of the Bozart."

Southerners and non-Southerners alike have become accustomed to the image of the Southerner as a bigoted, uneducated, rural boob. Both his prejudice and his incompetence are seen as cutting across social class lines; Senator Claghorn is hardly superior to Li'l Abner.

In the rest of the nation the image of the South altered from one of tragedy during the last third of the nineteenth century to that of a bad joke in the first third of the twentieth.

In the political arena, the Southern rhetoric concerning states' rights and independence from "federal interference" contributes to the bad joke. Other states contribute to the federal budget; the South is on the take. On the national average in 1968-69, the fifty states got 7.3 percent of their revenue for elementary and secondary schools from the federal government. But the South took 12.3 percent, led by such bastions of local autonomy as Alabama, Arkansas, and Mississippi with 15.9, 16.9, and 20.0 percent respectively. In the United States as a whole, state and local expenditures for public assistance from their own revenue sources ran to .74 percent of state personal income in 1968. The South contributes less than one-half the national average at .32 percent. During the same period, the Southern states' contributions to taking care of their own have decreased 17.9 percent. Only five states provide an average of less than $1,000 per year to support a family of four on welfare, and all five of them are in the South. As for public assistance expenditures, the average state receives 53.1 percent of its funds from the federal government. The only reason the national figure is that high is that the Southern states run almost 50 percent above the national average in federal dependency: Alabama, 76.0; Arkansas, 74.6; Florida, 74.8; Georgia, 76.5; Kentucky, 76.2; Louisiana, 72.5; Mississippi, 78.6; North Carolina, 71.0; South Carolina, 73.8; Tennessee, 74.9; Texas, 75.4; and Virginia, 64.8.

These kinds of figures are in some ways like the ghetto welfare and unemployment figures of Northern states. They are evidence not of stagnancy but of the drastic social dislocations arising from sudden rapid change. Joseph S. Vandiver says that "the plantation of Southern legend is gone for good," and Michael Aiken and N. J. Demerath, III. add that the South "has moved from plantations to poverty in the last century." Both the rural South and the urban North pay a considerable price for the technological revolution that is itself in major part a consequence of the incredible growth of farm productivity in the United States.

The explanation for the recency and suddenness of urbanization lies in the ratio of farmers to urban dwellers. Not until the industrial revolution with its factory systems, improved farming techniques, and tremendous speed-up of transportation of goods was it possible for whole societies to become urbanized. Technological advances diminish the need for farm laborers. In 1900 one farm worker's labor fed seven people. By 1950, one farm worker's labor fed nearly sixteen people. The latter figure more than doubled in fifteen years; by 1965 one farm worker's labor fed thirty-three people. The past twenty-five years have seen a greater technological revolution in rural America than in our mass production factories. Farm output by man hour has increased twice as fast as non-farm productivity. Much more can be produced with far fewer people, and this has meant endemic unemployment and underemployment in the most critically effected areas. Half the nation's poor families—and seven out of ten of the Negro poor families —live in the South.

As Michael Harrington says:

The old poor, who were typical up until the Thirties, lived at a time when economic opportunity was a secular trend of the economy itself. They suffered terribly, to be sure, and by objective indices of living standard and life expectance, most were worse off than the impoverished of 1968. But they also participated in that incredible growth of American capitalism, a development which, in Colin Clark's computation, saw a 4500 percent increase in the net income from manufacturing between 1860 and 1953. The farmers often came to the city in good times to better their luck. They were not driven into the metropolis as bewildered, despairing exiles, which is regularly the case today.

Arlyne I. Pozner discusses one of the prices of this migration in her chapter on "The Census Search for Missing Parents"—the "parentless" child left with grandparents or other relatives when the parents move North to the city.

During the first three centuries of Negro residence in the United States most black Americans were both Southerners and farmers. As recently as 1900, 90 percent of all black Americans lived in the South and 80 percent of all black people in the United States lived in rural areas. By 1950, 63 percent of all black Americans were urban dwellers. Outside the South over 90 percent lived in cities. In 1900, six states, all Southern, had populations that were over 35 percent Negro. By 1960, Mississippi was the only state where black people comprised more than 35 percent of the population.

Throughout American history the story of the South has been largely the story of the black American. It has not often been told that way, but it has certainly been acted out that way. In 1940, 77 percent of black Americans still lived in the South. By now nearly half live outside the South, but it is not surprising that the story of the civil rights protest movement was initially a Southern story.

Sociologists know that revolutions, whether peaceful or violent, are made not by most downtrodden and oppressed participants in a social order, but by those whose status has been improving and who then find that access to further improvement is blocked. This society become a nation when a revolution was organized by the thirteen best-governed colonies in the world. A few years later a revolution was made in France—not by serfs, but by the bourgeoisie. The civil rights protest movement of the 1950's and 1960's was led not by sharecroppers or by unemployed unskilled laborers but by clergymen, lawyers, and college students.

We, as social scientists, should not be thrown off the trail by the skillful press relations of a Bob Moses when he appears on television in his tattered sweater and overalls to talk about grass roots leadership. Moses is a leader all right; he is also the holder of an M.A. in philosophy from Harvard. It is not accidental that the early effective organization and vigorous protest occurred in the Deep South where the discrepancy was most marked between the achievement of middle-class characteristics, such as a college education, and the access to middle-class perquisites, such as respectful service in a restaurant.

It is one thing to live in a caste society where one is taught to expect to stay in his place, but black Americans have been taught—by schools, by churches, by patriotic pronouncements, and by the mass media—to expect the rewards available in an open competitive society and have been frustrated by the denial of these rewards.

As recently as 1950, eighteen states prohibited segregation in transportation and recreation facilities. Now the Interstate Commerce Commission has outlawed all racial barriers on trains and buses and in terminals.

Twenty years ago the white primary prevented the majority of Negroes from voting in the elections that counted in the South. The Supreme Court struck at white primaries in 1954, and in 1957 Congress passed the first civil rights act in eighty years, empowering the Justice Department to bring suits to win the ballot for Negroes. Voter registration has increased dramatically throughout the South since the passage of the 1965 voting rights act as evidenced in black political domination of such former white supremist strongholds as Fayette, Mississippi, and Green County, Alabama.

In 1950 there were more states in which segregation in the public schools was mandatory than there were states in which school segregation was prohibited. The Supreme Court outlawed public-school segregation in 1954. Today every state has begun at least token compliance with the order.

School desegregation in the South more than doubled between the school year 1965-66 and that of 1966-67. The percentage of black students attending desegregated schools changed in that year from an average for eleven Southern states of 6.1 percent to an average the next year of 15.9 percent. The issue, of course, is by no means settled. People are particularly likely to resist changes that they see as forced on their group by outsiders. As armies of occupation know (and as Americans have seen in the case of Office of Education guidelines for desegregation in the South), changes that seem to be imposed from the outside are likely to be greeted with overt compliance and covert resistance. When the Civil Rights Act of 1964 made it clear that school desegregation was not only a Court requirement but a national mandate, Southern politicians began to embrace a doctrine called "freedom of choice"— the right of every child, black or white, to choose the school he wants to attend. Acceptance of this doctrine hardly constituted the radical departure from Southern folkways that it might suggest if taken seriously as a slogan. Segregationist politicians had learned that freedom of choice did not bring a great deal of desegregation in such Deep South states as Mississippi. There, many blacks were afraid they would jeopardize their jobs and their personal safety if they enrolled their children in white schools. Also, of course, many feared the consequences, from loneliness to mistreatment, for their children. In those school districts where black parents applied for their children in large numbers, school officials simply turned many of them away on the ground that there was inadequate room for mass transfers into the white schools.

In 1969, a three-judge federal court panel in Jackson, Mississippi, upheld the freedom of choice plan for school desegregation in twenty-five school districts of southern Mississippi. A Supreme Court decision in 1968 had disapproved of freedom of choice if it were held by district courts to retard desegregation. The three-judge panel in 1969 said that "the freedom of choice plan in all of these cases is universally acclaimed by both races in all schools as being most desirable, most workable, and acceptable by everybody. Nobody testified to anything to the contrary or to anything better."

Another recent federal decision may slow the process of desegregation. Only 15 percent of the black students in Georgia attended predominantly white schools in 1968; this measure of desegregation had been achieved under threat by the Department of Health, Education and Welfare to cut off federal school funds. In August, 1969, the Department of Justice filed suit against the Georgia School Board to abolish its dual racial school system. In so doing, the Department relieved HEW of its enforcement role thus assuring that the local districts currently deprived of federal funds would receive them again until the issue is resolved in the courts, a procedure that could take years.

Northwestern University   *Raymond W. Mack*
Evanston, Illinois

Is the White Southerner Ready For Equality?

RAYMOND W. MACK

Two major issues with which the Kennedy administration must grapple bear a relationship to one another which is not visible at first glance. Significant progress in race relations—a matter of utmost urgency in both domestic and foreign policy—is closely linked to the whole question of federal aid to education. Neither civil rights legislation nor court decisions can provide a panacea for the problems of inequality between the races so long as we tolerate massive educational inequalities among the states.

In general, resistance to desegregation is highest where level of education is lowest. Industrial regions attract more people with more schooling than nonindustrial regions. Rural areas have lower average educational levels than urban areas, and rural people find rapid social change less congenial than urbanites do. The doctrine of massive resistance to the Supreme Court's desegregation decision has its roots and strength in the least industrialized, most rural

9

portion of the United States, the region where levels of formal education are lowest: the South.

During my brief tenure as assistant professor of sociology at the University of Mississippi a decade ago, I was struck by the sharp division of the faculty into two groups. Some —mostly young men, newly appointed, many in their first teaching post—oriented their thinking and their work toward the day when they would leave. The others were there to stay.

Those intending to leave were not a disgruntled or unhappy crew. They were scholars with a cosmopolitan view of the boundaries of their profession. To them, what was happening in physics or in psychology was more relevant than what was happening in Mississippi. They subscribed to national professional journals and presented research papers at national meetings.

For those who would stay put, the world was local, not cosmopolitan. Their significant "reference groups," as sociologists would say, were Mississippi and the South. I do not mean to make them sound like narrow, uneducated dunces; they were (and are) not. They were part of a university faculty, interested in painting, politics, music, writing and the exchange of ideas. But their dinner party discussions were likely to be devoted to topics with regional boundaries. What do you think of the new southern poet? Who are the most liberal southern Senators? Is the cultural life of Atlanta superior to that of New Orleans? What university has the strongest department of history in the South?

Even where they might come up with the same answers, the cosmopolitans and the locals phrased their questions differently. The former would ask who is the greatest contemporary American novelist; the latter would ask who is the greatest contemporary southern novelist.

The same choice of primary allegiance divided the student body. Most belonged to the group whose world was centered in Mississippi and bounded by the South. A markedly different few had their sights set on the time when, and the way in which, they would leave.

This division typifies the South as a whole. It represents the South's own problem, and the problem of the South as part of a larger nation. Some white southerners "pass" into the wider society. Others remain segregated within the only large, clearly-defined regional subculture in the United States. These locally oriented people are behaving exactly like what they are: a minority group.

So accustomed are we to thinking of minorities in racial and national terms—Italian-Americans, Negroes, Orientals, Jews, Polish-Americans—that it is easy for us to overlook the existence, much less the problems of our largest minority: the white southerners. By most criteria sociologists use in defining and studying minorities, white southerners are a minority.

A minority is stereotyped by the dominant group. Whether Jews, Negroes, or white southerners, they are thought of as a category sharing common characteristics and treated as a lump. Most Americans may expect one Oregonian to be different from another. But it is customary, even among editorial writers, columnists, and other intellectuals, to generalize about southerners. (Indeed, this is true to such an extent that it provides another example of the status of the American Negro as an "invisible man." When Americans say "southerner," they mean southern white.)

The southerner passes the ultimate test of the stereotype: people who do not conform to expectations are exempted from the category. Several times in social gatherings the turn of the conversation has led me to comment that my wife was born and reared in the South. The usual reassuring reply is, "Why, she doesn't seem like a southerner at all."

In the North, the statement, "You don't seem like a southerner" is invariably intended as a compliment. It is like saying, "She's a Jew, but she's very quiet"; or "He's a Negro, but a real gentleman." However, such generalizations about southerners are made by people who describe themselves as liberals and would be offended if accused of holding a stereotype of a racial or ethnic minority. But there is no better evidence of the existence of a stereotype than the need to exempt individuals from membership in their social category.

A minority is self-conscious. They are aware of the fact that the dominant group in their society views them as inherently different. They have mixed feelings of pride in their origins and defensiveness about the characteristics which set them apart. Irish-Americans boast to one another and kid among themselves about being hard-drinking fighters while resenting that public stereotype of Irish uncouthness. No other jokes contain the mixed tribal tenderness and vicious anti-Semitism of Jewish stories about Jewishness.

Southerners, too, know that they are scorned by other Americans. But who waves the Confederate flag at football games? One would be hard put to find a more potent example of paranoiac chauvinism that the best-selling (in Mississippi) automobile tags proclaiming: "Mississippi—the most lied-about state in the Union." The cross borne in the Bible Belt was described poignantly by the late poet-sociologist Howard Washington Odum of the University of North Carolina: "They used to hate us; now they laugh at us."

The way of life of a minority is viewed by others not as conforming to a set of standards with a value of its own, but as a measurable deviation from the "right way," the standards of the majority. It is an annoyance and a bother when a Jewish holiday falls on the day of college registration. Jewish students must be registered the day before or the day after everyone else. They cause trouble. Somehow registration does not happen to fall on Christmas or Easter. Similarly, in a university whose English department harbors defenders of the Third Edition of Webster's International Dictionary and teachers of the "usage, not rules" school of English, students with a southern accent take special corrective work in the School of Speech to learn to speak "correctly."

A minority is excluded from full participation in the society's business. The "balanced ticket" dear to the hearts of New York and Chicago politicians is not only a concession to minority power; it is evidence that the minority lacks true access to the power elite. We debated whether or not we could elect a Catholic president. No one raised seriously the question of whether we could elect as president a man really labelled a southerner. John Sparkman with Adlai Stevenson made a balanced ticket. But when Lyndon Johnson decided to try seriously for the top office, he and his supporters spent months creating an image of him as a Westerner and a national leader.

It is true, however, that white southerners enjoy influence and power in Congress very greatly out of proportion to their numbers, and in this way they differ from other minorities. Southern Congressmen are elected by small tightly-controlled electorates from which many whites as well as most Negroes are excluded (although these are counted in the census for determining numbers of "representatives"). They easily build up seniority over representatives more democratically elected and in greater danger of being defeated; by being secure in their offices southerners have come to dominate the majority of standing committees that actually control Congressional business. Even this great power, however, the South uses as an embattled minority would—mostly defensively, to stop what it doesn't want and to extract concessions and special privileges.

For the southerners are a minority. We stereotype them. They see themselves as different, and take pride in their race history and their ghetto. We are prejudiced against them. We discriminate against them.

While we are involved in a national effort to abolish residual slavery and raise the Negro American to the level of a full-fledged citizen, we tend to use the word "southerner" to connote someone oppressing a minority. But this should not blind us to the fact that the oppressors are themselves a minority.

We are committed to equality for the Negro. What about the southern white? Is he ready? Are we?

The resolution of this problem, like any minority problem, lies in the answer to the question: Can they be assimilated?

Assimilating southerners into American society will be a tremendous job. (I am now using that word to refer to locally and regionally oriented southerners. I am stereotyping and excluding those cosmopolitans who are already primarily Americans and only secondarily southerners.) The reason the South is hard to assimilate is not only that it has a distinctive history and culture. Goodness knows, southerners have participated in the country's crises; they have helped to make many and to solve others. The Mississippi National Guard, which was called upon to defend Mr. Meredith when he enrolled at Ole Miss, is proud of its record, and justifiably so. In the Korean War, it enlisted more volunteers and won more medals than any other state. But its pride is in the Mississippi National Guard, not in the United States.

The South has been largely excluded from the processes

Table 1.
STATE SPENDING FOR EDUCATION AND ITS CONSEQUENCES

Average Annual Expenditure for Education per pupil	State	Percentage of Population 18 years of age and over with less than 6 years schooling
Less than $200	Alabama	19.1
	Arkansas	18.0
	Georgia	20.6
	Kentucky	16.2
	Mississippi	22.0
	North Carolina	19.3
	South Carolina	23.8
	Tennessee	17.3
	Virginia	15.3
	West Virginia	12.9
$250-$249	Florida	10.8
	Idaho	3.9
	Louisiana	24.9
	Maine	5.5
	Nebraska	4.2
	Texas	15.7
	Vermont	4.4
$250-$299	Arizona	11.7
	Colorado	5.5
	Connecticut	7.4
	Kansas	4.3
	Illinois	7.4
	Iowa	3.5
	Maryland	9.0
	Massachusetts	7.0
	Michigan	6.8
	Nevada	4.6
	New Hampshire	5.2
	New Mexico	14.3
	North Dakota	7.0
	Ohio	6.3
	Oklahoma	10.1
	Pennsylvania	8.1
	Rhode Island	8.7
	South Dakota	4.8
	Washington	4.0
	Wisconsin	6.2

$300 or more	California	6.7
	Delaware	7.7
	Indiana	5.7
	Minnesota	4.7
	Missouri	8.3
	Montana	4.8
	New Jersey	8.2
	New York	9.1
	Oregon	3.9
	Utah	3.3
	Wyoming	4.2

which made the rest of America. The South remains predominantly agrarian, with a high birth rate and a low level of formal education. It is the most rural section of an urban society, the least schooled segment of an educated society, the least industrialized part of an industrial society. Historically, as Philip M. Hauser says, the North and West have been the productive parts of the United States, and the South has been the reproductive part.

Since the Supreme Court desegregation decision of 1954, many people have become familiar with the social science data on Army Alpha tests of intelligence by race and region. Whites from Arkansas, Kentucky and Mississippi scored significantly lower on these tests than Negroes from

Table 2.
THE NEGRO AND THE BALLOT IN THE SOUTH

State	Percentage of Negroes of Voting Age Who Are Registered to Vote
Alabama	12%
Arkansas	31
Florida	28
Georgia	22
Louisiana	26
Mississippi	5
North Carolina	28
South Carolina	13
Texas	31
Virginia	20

New York, Ohio and Illinois. These research results do not mean that southerners are innately inferior to northerners, any more than similar contrasts should be interpreted to mean that urbanites are smarter than farmers or that Negroes are inferior to whites. They simply emphasize the consequences of unequal educational opportunities. Seven years ago, ten states spent less than $200 per pupil on education, and every one of the ten was a southern state. At the same time, as Table 1 shows, 31 states spent $250 or more per pupil, and not one of them was in the South.

The products of these regional educational inequalities are immediately apparent in other statistics. Only eleven states in the continental United States have a rate of adult illiteracy of over 15 percent. Again, every one of them is in the South. This is one reason that literacy tests for voting can be skillfully used as instruments of racial discrimination in the South. Tennessee is the only state of the old Confederacy where as many as a third of the Negroes of voting age are registered to vote; the figure in Mississippi is 5 percent.

Table 3.
PROPORTION OF POPULATION IN COLLEGE, BY STATE, 1960

State	College Population as Percentage of Total Population Aged 18-24
Less than 20%	
Alabama	15.0
Arkansas	16.5
Delaware	18.9
Florida	16.0
Georgia	12.8
Kentucky	16.7
Louisiana	19.1
Maine	14.9
Maryland	19.4
Mississippi	17.1

Nevada	16.2
New Jersey	18.8
New Mexico	18.3
North Carolina	14.6
South Carolina	12.5
Tennessee	18.6
Virginia	14.0
West Virginia	19.0
20% to 26%	
Idaho	20.0
Illinois	24.1
Indiana	23.0
Iowa	25.1
Michigan	24.9
Missouri	22.4
Montana	22.9
New Hampshire	24.8
North Dakota	23.9
Ohio	21.4
Pennsylvania	21.4
Rhode Island	24.4
South Dakota	25.2
Texas	20.5
Wisconsin	23.3
Wyoming	23.5
26% and over	
Arizona	28.1
California	32.1
Colorado	29.2
Connecticut	26.4
Kansas	27.3
Massachusetts	31.3
Minnesota	26.7
Nebraska	28.0
New York	26.6
Oklahoma	27.2
Oregon	30.7
Utah	37.9
Vermont	30.0
Washington	26.7

Of the total population aged eighteen to twenty-four who were enrolled in college in 1960, we find nineteen states where the figure falls below 21 percent: the entire South, several border states, but only four states from all the rest of the country.

The social cost to the nation of this kind of inequality is documented in Melvin M. Tumin's study of what he calls "the hard core" of Southern resistance to desegregation. The outstanding characteristic of those most willing to resort to violence to defy the law of the land is a below-average amount of formal education. The violence-prone hard-core people belong to churches in about the same proportion as others and attend as frequently; they are as stable in residence patterns as their neighbors. But their earning power is significantly lower than that of their neighbors, and a much smaller percentage of them have completed nine years or more of school. As a result, the wider society impinges much less directly upon them; they are less influenced by the mass media of magazines, newspapers, radio, and television.

The trouble with a serious imbalance regionally in education and income is that it tends to feed upon itself. What is bad becomes worse precisely because it is known to be bad. A recent study by Russell Middleton, University of Wisconsin, shows that most department chairmen in southern colleges and universities believe that their recruiting of staff is hampered by the images scholars have of the South. Middleton's survey of doctoral candidates about to enter college teaching shows that the South is the last region where scholars choose to work. He concludes that "for the immediate future the prospects for higher education in the South are dubious."

They are likely to remain so until we accept the need to correct inequalities in the educational opportunities available to Americans, regardless of race, color, or region. It is difficult to see how we can achieve this if we cling to pathological fears of federal aid to education instead of using our federal government for what it is and should be: an instrument of our own will and destiny.

Americans have chosen to attack courageously the problem of unequal opportunities for Negro citizens. The task of redressing this shameful situation might be expedited by turning our attention at the same time to another culturally deprived minority.

November 1963

The Changing Realm
Of King Cotton

JOSEPH S. VANDIVER

"What would happen if no cotton was furnished for three years? England would topple headlong and carry the whole civilized world with her save the South. No, you dare not make war on cotton. No power on earth dares make war on cotton. Cotton is king!" thundered James H. Hammond of South Carolina in the United States Senate.

The year was 1858, and King Cotton was riding high. The South produced nearly four million bales of cotton that year. Since the invention of the cotton gin in 1793, the sleepy tempo of the Southern economy had quickened to a boom, and the moribund institution of slavery had revived to meet the vastly increased labor needs of the expanding plantations.

The planter himself lived in a state of luxury without prior parallel in American life. Stephen Duncan, a Mississippi planter of the 1850's, owned eight plantations, 1,018 field slaves, and 23 house slaves, and produced 4,000 bales

21

of cotton. His beautiful Greek Revival mansion near Natchez exemplified the legendary "Big House," its white pillars and porticos rising above the rolling green lawns and gardens that stretched for miles across the Mississippi countryside. Another planter, Greenwood Leflore, reputedly spent $10,000 to furnish one room of his mansion with imported Louis XIV chairs and sofas covered with gold leaf and crimson brocade.

"Great times in the Big House," recalled Isaiah Turner, a former Virginia slave. "Folks had plenty of money, and what they didn't buy, we raised for them. I remember the big parlor. Company come all the time, and the folks had big dinners. Fine ladies! Beautiful and they dressed like princesses. . . ."

The Civil War destroyed the institution of slavery which was so central to the entire plantation system. Many have chronicled the death of the Confederacy. However, what is not as well recorded is that, despite the devastation of the war, the plantations in the domain of King Cotton survived.

The green and white cotton fields of 1966 look much the same as those of 1859, but things have changed at the Big House. Morton Rubin, in his book, *Plantation County,* describes the living room of a contemporary Alabama plantation home:

None of the furniture in the room is older than twenty years. . . . The other rooms of the house—the dining room, electric kitchen, and bedroom upstairs—are too much like other American homes in the ten to twenty thousand dollar income class to warrant detailed description. . . . The house, like the plantation, is as modern as its owners can make it.

Despite the physical comfort, today's planter has little time to sit on the veranda sipping mint juleps. He is up at dawn, visiting the fields in his pickup truck or Land Rover and spending countless hours seeing that his tractors and mechanical harvesters are in good running order. He is a hard-working businessman managing an increasingly mechanized business. Cotton acreage had never risen much above the 10 million mark before the Civil War, but in 1930 the Southern soil was covered with 42 million acres of cotton. Today, improved agricultural methods have allowed Southern and Western cotton planters to reduce this acreage so that on one-third as much land they still produce about 15 million bales a year—nearly three times the amount produced in 1859, the peak year in pre-Civil War cotton production.

The plantation remains, but the system by which it operates, and the social corollaries of that system, have changed radically in the century since the end of the Civil War. How has King Cotton managed to survive? How has the transformation in his kingdom come about? And what effect has it had on the lives of his subjects—landowners and field hands alike?

After the Civil War, laborless planters and jobless Negroes came together to form a new system that was, in many respects, very like the old. The freed slave, now a "sharecropper," continued to live in a rent-free house on the planter's land and was paid for his labor not in regular wages, but by a share of the crop produced on the acreage designated as "his." The cropper was in theory free to leave at any time if he did not care to continue working for a particular planter, and the high rate of interplantation mobility indicates that many did move. But the fact remained that the sharecropper's freedom consisted almost entirely of freedom to move from place to place *within* the plantation network. Few were equipped by training or habit —or lured by the prospect of better opportunities elsewhere—to abandon the cotton fields altogether.

The sharecropping system had obvious advantages for the planter. First and foremost, it supplied cheap labor. In addition, it anchored the laborer and his family until 'settlement time" following the harvest; the cropper was not likely to leave the plantation before receiving his share of the year's profits. This assured the planter a guaranteed labor force and reduced the threat of interplantation competition for workers during "picking time" and other periods of peak demand. The cropper's interest in producing as much as possible on "his" acreage presumably motivated him to work hard. In bad years, the sharing system transferred some of the losses from the planter to the cropper.

The system also provided the planter with the opportunity to cheat his workers if he wanted to. The planter kept all the books concerning the operation, and the sharecropper had neither the education nor the legal protection to take issue with the planter's calculation of his share.

A side benefit for the planter was his operation of the plantation store. The sharecroppers could buy there on extended credit—but often at interest rates as high as 10 to 25 percent. Planters have defended this system on the grounds that their customers were very poor credit risks, but it is certain that the plantation commissaries were in business to make money as well as to provide a service for the Negro tenants of the plantation.

The sharecropping system also had advantages, though less obvious ones, for the newly emancipated Negro. The foremost was probably security. The system provided him a house, enough land to raise his own food, and enough credit at the plantation store to buy what he could not raise. It provided him the security of being retained throughout the season. And it allowed him to continue doing the kind of field work with which he was familiar.

At the same time, it gave him a sense of independence to have a certain acreage set aside as "his," which he could work as he pleased without the direct supervision of a white overseer. The freed Negro's reluctance to work as a laborer in a gang, so reminiscent of slavery, appears to have survived even today in plantation areas of the Deep South. Harold A. Pedersen, in an article on attitudes toward modernization in the Delta, relates a story told to him by a planter who was having trouble getting Negro men to work as tractor drivers on his newly mechanized plantation, despite the lure of higher pay.

As the story goes, a planter who planned to go fishing asked a small Negro boy how much he would charge to row the boat. The boy replied, "Two dollars," and the planter agreed. After they were out in the boat, however, the planter began to think that the price was unusually high, and asked the boy how much he was paid for his regular work at the local bait store. "One dollar," was the reply. Realizing that the planter expected some further explanation, the boy went on: "Well, you see, Mr. Joe (the owner) is in and out, but when you and me are out in that boat you're there looking at me all the time." The Negro tractor driver too works under the unblinking gaze of a white supervisor who is "there looking at him all the time," and he too dislikes it.

In addition to freedom from constant supervision, sharecropping had other advantages in the eyes of plantation Negroes. Most important were the eternal hope of a really good year and the certain and defined access to "furnish" from the landlord. Under the "furnish" system, the planter provided the cropper with the farm tools and implements necessary for his work plus a restricted credit for some food during the cold season and occasional extras such as tobacco and work clothes. One observer noted that the very fact that the planter provided each cropper with a mule was a lure; the animal was used for work, to be sure, but it also provided transportation to church, to town, and to the fishing stream. This "furnish" supplied by the landlord was considered an advance against the proceeds of that cropper's share, and the opportunity for dishonest book-keeping thus provided the planter with yet another chance to cheat the cropper.

Thus the sharecropping system assured the planter his traditional supply of black field labor and assured the former slave his traditional access to food and shelter pro-, vided by the white man. The paternal role of the planter and the dependant role of the Negro field hand were basically unaltered. The sharecropping arrangement set the mold of stratified plantation society more firmly than ever, until the tradition-shattering days of the Great Depression.

By 1930, 25 percent of all farm operators and 44 percent of all tenant farmers in the South were sharecroppers. Most of these—particularly in cotton plantation areas—worked under some such arrangement as the "standard" share-cropping pattern described above. Certain variations on the theme emerged in some parts of the South, however.

In the 1920's, a quasi-sharecropping system had deveolped in the Corpus Christi area of Texas. It later spread to the Mississippi Delta and throughout the cotton country of the Southeast. Under this system, the worker became part labor-er and part cropper—usually more the former than the latter, though he was likely to be statistically classified as a sharecropper. A small acreage which he and his family worked on shares immobilized him through the season, but much of the time he worked as a day hand on acreage unas-signed to shares. Various modifications emerged; some plan-tations assigned workers exclusive rather than shared bene-fits from very small tracts, a system reminiscent of the *mini-*

fundia arrangements of Colombia and other parts of Latin America. Or, as plantations become increasingly mechanized, tractor drivers, who were needed constantly during the season, might be anchored by shares assigned to their families.

In 1930, however, mechanization still seemed far away, and the traditional system of sharecropper field labor was the accepted arrangement on most plantations. Then came the depression. Planters had to cut back on the number of workers they could maintain, and many sharecroppers were turned off the land they had come to regard as their own. Unemployment spiralled, and labor agitation was in the air. The first sharecroppers' union sprang up in Tallapoosa County, Alabama, in 1931. It was organized by industrial workers who stressed the hardships of the depression to kindle grievances among the Negro croppers who had been or faced the threat of being displaced from the land.

In 1934, the Southern Tenant Farmers Union was organized in Arkansas. It challenged cotton country tradition not only by the mere fact of its existence, but by being bi-racial —an alliance of the Negro and the poor white. Retribution was swift and merciless, making the brief career of the STFU one of the bloodiest episodes in the history of American unionism. Howard Kester, one of the leading organizers of the STFU, described the situation in his 1936 book, *Revolt Among the Sharecroppers:*

> While violence of one type or another has been continually poured out upon the membership of the union . . . it was in March 1935 that a "reign of terror" ripped into the country like a hurricane. For two-and-a-half months, violence raged through northeastern Arkansas and in neighboring states. . . . Meetings were banned and broken up; members were falsely accused, arrested and jailed, convicted on trumped-up charges and thrown into

prison; relief was shut off; union members were evicted from the land by the hundreds; homes were riddled with bullets from machine guns; churches were burned and schoolhouses stuffed with hay and floors removed; highways were patrolled night and day by armed vigilantes looking for the leaders; organizers were beaten, mobbed and murdered until the entire country was terrorized.

Kester describes the famous STFU strike of 1936:

On a given night the strike bills were distributed throughout the territory. So effectively were they distributed that many people thought an airplane had dropped them down on the cabins. On the following day, a strange emptiness hung over the cotton fields. Most of the workers did not go to the fields, and those who did soon returned to their cabins. . . . A labor official from Little Rock made a trip through the cotton country to see how effective the strike was. He reported that he saw two workers picking cotton. The strike was effective, and the cotton hung in the bolls until the union told the men to go back to work.

The STFU eventually foundered, but the Delta would never be the same again. The mold had begun to crack. In the decades that followed, three forces—acreage restriction, Negro emigration from the South, and mechanization—were to revolutionize the cotton kingdom.

When, starting in 1933, the Agricultural Adjustment Administration (AAA) restricted cotton acreage, plantation labor demands were further reduced. Some planters retained their croppers even though there was little work for them to do. Others, feeling the pinch, cut their labor force again and turned more croppers off the land. Shrewd croppers often used their persuasive powers to obtain enough "furnish" to end the season in debt, assuming that the planter would retain those croppers who owed him money.

Acreage restrictions not only reduced the total labor needs of the plantation, but also encouraged a shift from sharecropping to wage labor. Government payments for acreage restrictions, soil conservation, and the soil bank required division of receipts between owner and tenant. The sharecropper, defined as tenant, was thus eligible for such payments, but landowners operating the entire establishment as a unit employing wage labor had the right to unshared retention of the government money.

By transferring their laborers from a sharecropping to a wage basis, and by other legal maneuvers, many planters were able to cheat their tenants out of AAA payments. A government research team found, in 1936, that landlords had received an average of $822 per plantation, compared with $108 per plantation for *all* the tenants put together. As observers Fred S. Frey and T. Lynn Smith accurately remarked at the time, the AAA program had turned out to be no more than "a mere subsidy to planters."

The reduced rate of Negro migration from the South during the 1930's, combined with the reduced need for plantation labor under the acreage restriction program, led to a labor surplus. This situation further aided the planters in monopolizing AAA payments, since they did not have to offer a crop share in order to get workers. But in forsaking the customary sharecropping arrangement for the express purpose of profiting at the tenant's expense, the landlord was contributing to a breakdown of a way of life. Not only did his action alter the external economic relationship between the Big House and the field workers, but it contributed to the growth of mistrust and hatred among the already destitute black laborers of the cotton country. No longer could the planter be counted upon to provide for "his people."

Many planters retained workers they did not need during the depression and gave their sharecroppers a fair share of the AAA payments. But when World War II broke out, even these sharecroppers left the land by the thousands to join the armed forces or to take well-paid jobs in the urban war-industry centers.

During the decade between 1940 and 1950, well over one million Negroes left the South. The state of Mississippi alone lost an estimated 258,000—many of them share-croppers and their families. They headed for the big industrial centers of the North and the West—for New York, Chicago, Detroit, and Los Angeles. Between 1940 and 1950, state-by-state estimates show that the Negro population increased by 243,000 in New York; by 193,000 in Michigan; by 180,000 in Illinois; and by 259,000 in California.

Once started, the pattern of migration seemed self-perpetuating. The Negro exodus from the South not only continued, but, according to most estimates, increased during the period from 1950 to 1960. During this time, the state of Mississippi lost some 264,000 Negroes—several thousand more than in the preceding decade. Again, it is evident that a large proportion of these people were plantation field laborers and their families.

Part of the reason for this continuing migration may have been the government's re-imposition of cotton acreage restrictions during the 1950's. Employment opportunities for unskilled labor were shrinking in the North after the war ended, but they were shrinking even more rapidly in the plantation areas of the South. An additional 243,000 Negroes poured into New York state (mostly into the ghettos of Harlem and Bedford-Stuyvesant in New York City) ; 159,000 into Illinois; 110,000 into Michigan; and 220,000 into California.

Plantation mechanization in the cotton country, even more than renewed acreage restriction, reduced work opportunities and spurred continuing Negro migration during the 1950's. Many planters had mechanized during the war to escape dependence on an unsure labor force. Others expressed bitterness over having been left short of hands during the 1940's after they had retained extra workers during the depression out of a sense of paternalistic responsibility. Now they no longer felt compunctions about replacing men with machines.

A circular situation developed; departing workers encouraged mechanization, and mechanization encouraged workers to leave. To the extent that laborers viewed mechanization as inevitable, decisions about migration may have been influenced in advance of actual mechanization on their own plantations. Planters sometimes purchased machines to use if needed, leaving them idle as long as workers were still there; an unused mechanical picker in the machine shed could in itself be a powerful factor inducing the remaining workers to accept whatever terms were available.

By the 1950's, it was evident that weed control, rather than harvesting, was the final challenge to be overcome for full mechanization of cotton production in the humid Southeastern climate. Most planters felt that checkerboard planting, the rotary plow, and the flamethrower, while useful, could not be depended on in wet years to control the growth of weeds. Thus a certain labor reservoir of weed choppers was needed. With these people on hand, there was a tendency to use them for a variety of operations, so many planters ran a less mechanized business than existing skill and equipment made possible.

By the end of the 1950's, such partial mechanization reached into all portions of the cotton belt. The process started earlier and advanced more rapidly in the Delta areas of Arkansas, Mississippi, and Louisiana than elsewhere. In every area, it advanced unevenly. Harold A. Pedersen and Arthur F. Raper tell the story of "Tractor Plantation" where the entire operation was mechanized except for two tenant tracts, still farmed with mules in the old way; the occupants had been on the plantation a long time and were permitted to remain, undisturbed by the transformation under way around them.

Under the impact of partial mechanization, sharecropping receded rapidly in the latter part of the 1950's. Bolivar County, Mississippi, which had 10,643 sharecropping units in 1930, reported only 975 in the 1959 Census of Agriculture. Plantations have always used casual labor from nearby towns and cities during periods of peak demand, but, with the reduced working force on the land, such labor has become relatively more important. These day workers are sometimes recruited by "truckers" who haul them to the plantations; the wise planter seeks the cooperation of a dependable trucker to maintain an adequate labor supply.

Very recently, the last barriers to full mechanization have been giving way. In 1962, about 75 percent of the cotton in the Delta areas of Mississippi and Louisiana was harvested mechanically. More important, the chemical breakthrough in weed control by the use of herbicides promises to be effective enough and inexpensive enough to clear the remaining bottleneck to complete mechanization. Widespread adoption of herbicides is now occurring, particularly in the Delta.

As plantations come to rely upon mechanization and wage labor for their operations, they are evolving a new institutional structure and new occupational roles. The modern plantation is a small bureaucracy, with laborers working under a labor supervisor and with machine operations under the "manager." The fact that the title of "manager" goes to the man with responsibility for the machines suggests where the greatest importance is placed. Workers with a problem go to their supervisor; on the traditional plantation, the owner was personally accessible to the workers and handled their requests directly.

All indications suggest that the mechanization process is now accelerating in plantation areas, particularly in the Mississippi Delta. There is no indication that the final stages of mechanization are required because of lack of labor. Rather the impetus and the irreversibility of the process itself seem to be involved. There is little basis to assume, optimistically, that its completion will be painless to those Negroes who are providing the field labor still utilized.

In early June of 1965, the ghost of the depression-spawned STFU stirred, and the first plantation strike in three decades hit the Mississippi Delta. The STFU's successor was the Mississippi Freedom Labor Union, organized in close alliance with the cotton-belt civil rights movement.

Challenging the white overlords of the Delta's quarter-of-a-billion-dollar-a-year cotton industry, Negro plantation workers struck for higher wages. The tractor drivers were only receiving $6 for a 14-hour day, and $3 for a 10-hour day was the going rate for weed choppers (mostly the wives and children of the tractor men). The workers demanded $1.25 per hour for both drivers and choppers.

The planters were adamant in their refusal to give in to the union demands. "Wages are really too high now," said one planter, "because we don't really need hand labor. We could do the job better, quicker, and cheaper with machinery and chemicals." The implication was clear; the weed choppers, by striking, were only hastening their own replacement by angering the planters into full and immediate mechanization.

Current labor agitation in the Delta, like that of the 1930's, reflects the existence of a labor surplus combined with diminishing opportunities for employment. Contrary to the trend from 1930 to 1960, recent population estimates in the Delta and "brown loam" plantation counties of Mississippi indicate that, since 1960, the number of nonwhites in this area has remained stationary or has actually increased. Other figures, which are not broken down by race, show that the state lost a total of only 12,000 people in the period 1960-1963; even if we assume that all of these 12,000 were Negro, this figure is well below the three-year average for Negro migration out of Mississippi for any period since 1940. More complete data are lacking, but it appears that, if Negro migration from the cotton country has indeed slowed down to this degree—presumably as a result of the current weakness of the "pull" of Northern metropolitan areas for non-whites of low skill—then a marked piling up of young adults must be occurring at the very time that agricultural wage labor is being replaced by herbicides and mechanical picking.

This labor situation will undoubtedly exercise a powerful effect on the nature of the civil rights movement in the plantation areas of the South. These areas are already islands of poverty in the Southern countryside. In 10 typical cotton counties of Alabama, Arkansas, Louisiana, Mississippi, North Carolina, and South Carolina, 61 percent of the residents in 1959 were nonwhites; of these, 44 percent received a family income of less than $1,000 for the year, and fully 90 percent received less than $3,000. What will happen as the current wave of social protest penetrates this group, whose already precarious livelihood is now in danger of being cut off altogether by the advent of tractors and weed killers in the cotton fields?

The 1965 protests of the Mississippi Freedom Labor Union and the responsiveness of many Negroes in the area to the theme of "black power" in 1966 offer hints of what may come. The under-employed Negroes in the poverty areas of the cotton belt find migration unpromising, have plenty of time to demonstrate, and have little to risk by doing so. As one young MFLU striker was quoted in *Newsweek*: "We ain't got nothin', so we ain't got nothin' to lose."

This much is certain—fewer and fewer young Negroes will wind up spending their lives as plantation field hands, picking cotton and chopping weeds. The plantation of Southern legend is gone for good. Whether or not the large tracts of machine and chemical cultivated acreage that are now emerging will still be called "plantations," and whether or not their operators invest themselves with the sentimental trappings of the old order, the transition will likely be a painful one.

November 1966

FURTHER READING SUGGESTED BY THE AUTHOR:

Southern Tradition and Regional Progress, by William H. Nicholls. Chapel Hill, N. C.: University of North Carolina Press, 1960.
Mississippi: The Closed Society, by James Wesley Silver. New York: Harcourt, Brace and World, 1966.
The New Revolution in the Cotton Economy, by James Harry Street. Chapel Hill, N. C.: University of North Carolina Press, 1957.

The Politics of Tokenism in Mississippi's Delta

MICHAEL AIKEN/N. J. DEMERATH III

"The real choice is whether we're going to obey the law with federal aid or obey the law without federal aid. If we sit back and say 'Make us, sue us' we would be faced with real administrative chaos."

White school board president

"Those of you who do not want to send your children to school with niggers, get out and vote against those liberals and cheap politicians who would jeopardize your child's future."

Midnight leaflet from White Voters League

"So far it's been a honest-to-God miracle. There ain't been any real troubles; our kids has been treated pretty well. It can be did, but it's just beginning and the real trouble ain't even begun yet."

Parent of Negro child in a white school

With more of a whimper than a bang school desegregation came to much of Mississippi in the fall of 1965. This is a report on its problems—milder so far than expected—and its prospects—hazy but hardly rosy. To date there have been few "incidents." But there are also very few

Negro children in white schools and no white children in Negro schools.

This report is based on two different districts in the Mississippi Delta. One is a growing town of about 40,000, with a cosmopolitan elite tradition. The other is a rural county containing a host of small towns, still encapsulated within the "closed society." We have called the one "River City," the other "Bayou County." However different from each other, they represent neither all of Mississippi nor even all of the Delta itself. The study's data consist of interviews. But it was not always easy to know whom to interview and harder still to know whom to believe. Talk about racial matters is not cheap with either Mississippi whites or Negroes, let alone both on a single visit. Elected officials are public relations specialists; dissidents bloat their complaints out of proportion; and the mythical "average citizen" usually cares little and knows less.

Throughout we have changed the names of places and people to protect the guilty as well as the innocent. This is itself a commentary on the open wounds of the Deep South. Our intention was not to act as Feds, finks, or petti-foggers. Yet even the results of anonymous research can be harsh.

Nothing at all can be understood out of context, and the present context has moved from plantations to poverty in the last century. The Mississippi Delta is the blackest part of the Black Belt—black as to soil, people, and current prospects. It is a half moon of rich alluvial land where cotton, levees, and the labor of Negro slaves once brought wealth to a plantation aristocracy. But King Cotton has been brought to his knees. Mechanization and increasingly rigid federal acreage controls have destroyed a way of life. Planters, small farmers, and sharecroppers have all suffered. Negro laborers, for whom the plantation system was a curse, are now the victims of yet another scourge.

It was estimated that half the 25,900 Negro cotton pickers and choppers in the Delta would lose their jobs between 1965 and 1966. True they earn only $3 for a 12-14 hour shift. But there is no money elsewhere. Welfare payments in Mississippi average $2.50 a week and are only for children, the old, and the handicapped.

One solution is to leave, and many do. Currently Mississippi has a population of just over two million—1.2 million of its native born are living elsewhere, one-fifth of them in Illinois, especially the slums of Chicago. Between 1950 and 1960, 137,426 people, mostly Negroes, left the Delta, bringing the proportion of Negro residents down from a high of 85 percent at the apex of the plantation system to a current 65 percent.

Industry has moved in to take advantage of cheap labor, tax concessions, and a hospitable climate. Still, its employees are almost exclusively white because of both discrimination and the nature of the potential Negro work force —untrained, and in many cases untrainable. In 1960 over half the Delta Negroes had less than five years of schooling. Less than 5 percent had finished high school.

It is to people in this hopeless condition that the civil rights movement is making its appeal. At the very least it is a new romance doing battle with the outdated plantation mythology. Insofar as Negroes support "the movement," they do so out of desperation. One displaced Negro laborer said about Northern civil rights workers: "These people are down here to help people like me. I ain't got nothing at all to lose by joining."

Still, there are differences in social climate within the area. River City is relatively prosperous and progressive, with a tradition of cultural sophistication and even racial moderation. There is a social distinction here between the white elite and the "redneck" or "peckerwood" families. By contrast, there is little such distinction in Bayou County where the rednecks *are* the elite. The county is tied more firmly to the crumbling cotton economy and has more Negroes and more poverty.

The distinction is reflected in the schools of the two areas. River City has always been proud of its schools. A local historian wrote in 1912, "The River City schools have always been second to none in the state, and the graduates are admitted without examination into the universities of the different states." But in 1912 there were only a few public schools for whites in Bayou County, and those for Negroes developed later and at random. These are hardly a source of pride by any pedagogic standard.

Compliance in River City

"The time has come for footdragging public school boards to move with celerity toward desegregation. The rule has become: the later the start, the shorter the time for transition."

> *Judge J. Minor Wisdom, U. S. Court of Appeals for the Fifth Circuit, June 30, 1965, Jackson, Miss.*

The above ruling reflects the increased pressure from the federal courts to speed Mississippi school desegregation. This pressure has been crucial. Without it, there would not even be token desegregation in the state today. Most school districts have been waiting since 1954 and the Supreme Court decision for the federal lightning to strike them specifically. The storm intensified with the civil rights bill of 1965, but few made any preparations for what was nearly inevitable. It is true that some districts are still waiting for compulsion, but most, like Bayou County, have fallen victim to a court order late and unprepared.

River City was an exception. Along with a few other

school systems, it decided to stay a jump ahead of the Feds, mainly to guard its federal educational funds. Although the first River City voluntary segregation plan of February 1965 fell far short of US Office of Education requirements, it was nonetheless hailed locally as a bold move. "This is no time," trumpeted a local paper, "for the faint of heart to sit on any Deep Southern school board." And in May 1965 registration of grades one and two only was held for the following September, on a "freedom of choice basis" whereby any student could register for any school, Negro or white.

The registration went smoothly, but two grades were not enough to satisfy federal standards. In June, the courts upset the strategy of "underintegration" by ordering the Jackson, Mississippi, schools to observe the full Office of Education requirement and desegregate four specified grades in September. Flustered but game, the River City bureaucrats fell in line with the decision, knowing it would reach them soon anyway. They added the seventh and twelfth grades to their plan, thus bringing it in line with federal requirements, except that the already registered second grade was substituted, by permission, for the specified tenth.

As in May, August registration was virtually uneventful, though only 147 Negroes out of a possible 1,500 chose white schools. By the following January the number of Negroes still attending those schools had dropped to 121. Note, however, that this was not due to official pressure to switch back to Negro schools, common in some "desegregated" districts. According to the River City superintendent:

> We just put our foot down and said, "Brother, you chose to go to a white school and now you're going to." I don't care what color a student's skin is, white, black,

purple, or orange—I'm not going to run an educational cafeteria on a short order basis.

No, indeed. Negroes unhappy in the white schools simply dropped out altogether, like an estimated 22,000 other school-age children in Mississippi. The state's compulsory attendance law was never enforced, and it was formally revoked on the heels of the Supreme Court schools decision.

The Negroes that remained in the white River City schools confronted no acute problems. Even the reputed local leader of the United Klans of America admitted, perhaps disappointedly, that everyone behaved nicely. Little was made of the few mild incidents that did occur, such as a little white first-grade girl being kissed by a Negro classmate. Although Negro students were sometimes shoved in the halls amid audible mutterings of "Nigger," their parents had expected far worse.

But desegregation, however uneventful, is a far cry from real integration. Only the smaller children were friendly across the racial barrier. At the high school, even the one cherished example of student acceptance turned out to have its less acknowledged seamy side. The nomination of a Negro student as vice president of the dramatics club was later cancelled by the high school principal, "to save the boy from intended embarrassment," as the principal explained at awkward length. Since the boy was one of the most popular Negro students in the school, it is just possible that the election was on the level and the concern for embarrassment was more projected than altruistic.

Still, even militant civil rights leaders admitted that the teachers did not discriminate socially or in their grading. Unhappily, this fairness did not save the Negro students from academic failure. They did poorly all around, worse in the upper grades than the lower, and worst of all in examinations. At the junior high level, the Negroes made up 15 percent of the student body but 47 percent of the failures. The situation was worse in the high schools where the Negroes opted out of pride and despite counselling for the stiff college preparatory curriculum. In all of this, poor home environment was a factor, but even more important was the poor quality of the Negro schools the students came from. The older students fared worse because they had longer exposure to the crippling Negro schools. Indeed, even the River City school administrators now admit that the notion of "separate but equal" schools is a guilt-allaying myth. But the most important factor in the poor performance of the Negro students, particularly in the high school, was that the brightest Negroes did not opt for white schools. As we shall see later, they had too much to lose by switching.

The poor academic performance of the Negro students was a shock to many people, including the more liberal white teachers. River City High's prize history teacher, Mr. Bernstein, had already had experience with what he called "technicolor education." He originally had no qualms about lowering the standards of his advanced seminar to admit a Negro girl. But she could not keep up, and he wonders whether the choice is not between seeming discrimination and long-term academic decline. This is only one of several dilemmas still confronting River City's gallant but only partly successful attempts to desegregate.

Now let us look at school desegregation in Bayou County—the more typical Mississippi response.

Resistance in Bayou County

"I don't know many school people who were really hostile towards the plan, but the fact is we just weren't ready."

County Superintendent of Schools

"If we didn't have to do it overnight it would be easier. If I was on the other side of the fence, I'd understand how they [the Negroes] feel. We had 100 years to do something for them and we didn't."

White high school principal

On August 24, 1965, barely a week before school opened, the US district judge ordered the schools of Bayou County to desegregate at least four grades, including the first, by the 1965-1966 school year. There had been no last ditch efforts to ward off the blow, nor, as in River City, to prepare for it. In the absence of a county plan, individual school systems made their own choices as to which three grades, in addition to the first, would be desegregated. Most opted for the last three years of high school, because, as we shall explain, they could be sure of few takers. One nearby county in a similar fix opened all 12 grades to Negroes in a gesture of total resignation, but this was unique.

Bayou County's "freedom of choice" registrations occurred only a few days after the court directive. Phalanxes of special policemen were on duty to ward off incidents and perhaps symbolically to ward off Negroes as well. Negro applicants for white schools were rigorously screened. One small town official remarked:

There were 15 Negroes who qualified and registered. I know they qualified because there was enormous political pressure put on the school board to have them disqualified. I certainly wouldn't have checked 15 white students so closely.

Naturally enough there were few applicants—only 48 or about 2 percent of those eligible, although nearly 75 percent of the county's schoolchildren are Negro. The Negro community was not only scared, but it was even less prepared than the whites. One civil rights leader hinted that the court order might have been issued late on purpose, to give them no time to organize. Certainly the decision fell short of the original suit that had asked for more desegregation than four grades and the desegregation of the faculty as well. Many Negroes felt that an elephant had labored to deliver a white mouse. Several schools in the county managed to "escape" Negro students altogether.

Those Negro students who did attend white schools were received with noticeable lack of enthusiasm, though without violence. White teachers were uncomfortable, and a few threatened to quit—no light matter in Mississippi where the startlingly low salaries make recruitment and replacement difficult. Administrators were in a barely controlled panic. One principal gathered his seven Negro students, all girls, and lectured them on how to avoid trouble—by acting like Jackie Robinson! The general assumption was that the Negroes were the potential troublemakers. As one official said, "We haven't had trouble between the races in this area. Our leaders of the Negro people have controlled this thing." Within the schools, Negro students were given a collective cold shoulder. A white school principal reported, with a mixture of concern and satisfaction, "At our high school they get the 'deep freeze treatment.' Not one white student has spoken to them. It's been 100 percent." Originally, a few white students were friendly to the Negroes, but they were soon taught better by their peers and parents.

In high school, the girls were better received than the boys. This is no surprise since Mississippi whites have always regarded the young Negro male as a potential troublemaker and a fabled threat to white virginity. In any case, few boys even made the switch to white schools. In this state, Negro boys who stay in high school are often pursuing either academic or athletic scholarships. Both would be imperiled in a white school, because of higher academic standards and nonintegrated sports.

As to actual "trouble" in the more rural Bayou County, it varied from town to town. In "Bayou City," the largest and most civilized town in the county, "incidents" were fairly rare. In "Raeford," a civil rights hot spot since 1964, they were too numerous to list. We heard complaints about unfair grading by teachers (an unusual charge) as well as about wage cuts, firings, evictions, and other reprisals against Negro parents. "But," said a Raeford school principal smugly, "there's been no knifings or violence or that sort of thing." Apparently it would take a lynching to count as a reprisal in Raeford. It was here, incidentally, that a school official told us, "We don't have many Negroes in Raeford. Most of ours are niggers." He made it plain he was talking about poverty and immorality. Still the term is less usual these days. Elsewhere we heard only a carefully pronounced "Negro," and even the once sophisticated "Nigra" has been purged from the white vocabulary, at least for conversation with Northern social scientists.

One unmourned casualty of school desegregation in Raeford was the local PTA. In River City, Negro parents went to PTA meetings, but in Bayou City they prudently stayed away. In Raeford, however, the organization was simply disbanded. A white official made the surprising comment that it was no loss—it was run by John Birch types anyway.

As in River City, the Bayou County Negro students made poor grades in the white schools. Again, however, these were not the "best" Negro students. There is probably a good deal of truth in the allegation that the Negroes in the white high schools were more interested in civil rights than education. One Bayou County white administrator stated flatly:

All of the Negro students in the white schools come from hard core, militant families. If there are any superior students they are still over at the Negro high school. Certainly several of the Negro high school students had participated in and been arrested for civil rights work in the state. One can well imagine that civil rights work and formal educational pursuits often conflict. It is even more plausible that a zeal for civil rights is necessary to brave the hazards of Bayou County desegregation. And yet an elementary school principal gave the point a different cast:

Everybody around here thinks that the Negro parents are being paid to send their children to white schools. I doubt it, but it might be. I do know that the parents are the raunchiest you've ever seen. They have no sense of responsibility or cooperation.

He showed us the following letter from a Negro mother, asking for a parent-teacher conference, which, incidentally, was never held. It is unconvincing evidence of "raunchiness." But it does point to Bayou County's past educational failures and future challenges.

hello Mrs. Cheek

Reason I amm writting you to let you no can I make a pearmont With you and the principal monday about five minute tree oclock I want to talk to you about my daughter Linda

From Lind Mother, Luva Lloyd Minor

The Blessings of Bureaucracy

"Throughout the whole desegregation thing a lot of us white school people haven't been able to go as far and as quick as maybe we'd like to. It probably would have been easier to do it all at one time and get it over with. But just try convincing the school board of that."

White Bayou County high school principal

Successful desegregation is like making a good omelette. Both require the breaking of "eggs" and delicacy in the midst of heat. Both court disaster as ingredients separate. In this section we shall suggest some reasons why the first course in River City was somewhat more palatable than that in Bayou County. There will be no pointless talk about "good guys" and "bad guys." Instead we shall explore such conditioning circumstances as Delta politics, bureaucracy in the schools, and the civil rights movement within the Negro community. There will be no attempt to explain events through a single monolithic and malevolent "power structure." Instead, we will seek out structural variables that make for differences in the amount of power and the way it is exercised.

Mississippi has never been accused of leading the nation in such new-fangled administrative gimmicks as centralization. County rights are as revered as states' rights, especially in education. That state's education system is controlled, by and large, by rural district supervisors who run their bailiwicks like satraps. They and the local and county school boards are responsible only to a highly select electorate. One Negro civil rights activist and registered voter in Bayou County had no idea when school elections were held, let alone how.

Again, however, River City offers an important exception. Here the school board is appointed by the city fathers rather than elected "at large." In affording protection from local constituencies, it provides the board with crucial autonomy and anonymity in running the school system on its own terms. It also allows the board to follow the predilections of the elite it represents. River City's economic elite have both assumed and been pushed into behind-the-scenes political leadership during the civil rights crisis. The most prominent is a lawyer with distinguished family

connections and a chatty, even hip, conversational style.
Wilbur Cobb luxuriates in candor as much as wealth:

> You certainly can't account for desegregation here by
> the conscience of the local citizens. Most of us acted
> out of necessity rather than moral principles.

Or, more personally and more poignantly:

> The biggest sin the whites have committed against the
> Negroes . . . is the denial of human dignity. Yeah, that's
> the mama sin.

To moderates—perhaps even liberals—like Cobb, federal civil rights legislation offered relief to sore consciences.
Guilt over segregation had been festering for years, but
they were unable to take integrating initiative by themselves. Now they had only to urge compliance with the
law, a more temperate counsel. Soon after the civil rights
bill of 1964 was passed, 15 such men began to meet
regularly but covertly to smooth the transition. Negro leaders were not included, but they knew and called the group
"the Friday evening tea club." Once considered radicals
by the rest of the white community, the tea club had under-
gone a recent change in status. By contrast with the Northern civil rights workers who began to flood the town,
they became voices of reason, persons to be trusted with
planning the changes that were necessary. The middle
class Negro leadership also gained by comparison with
the outside civil rights workers, and slowly the local high-
status whites and Negroes began to coordinate their efforts.

In Bayou County, by contrast, the civil rights movement
disrupted the community instead of unifying it. Its small
towns had neither a white nor a Negro elite that might
cooperate. Lacking moderate leadership the two sides drew
back into their separate corners, like boxers waiting for
the bell. Even the once typical residential mingling of
Negroes and rednecks has declined since it now carries

the name of "integration." Moderates, if any, are locked away from one another in a general conspiracy of silence. Indeed, silence is crucial in maintaining the "closed society." One could wildly imagine a town in which every white citizen is a private integrationist but convinced that he is the only one and cowed by the prospects of going against the traditional tide. The image is far-fetched but provocative.

One important difference between the River City schools and those in Bayou County is that the former are more bureaucratized and run by professionals on the way up, while the latter are less bureaucratized and run by men now stripped of professional ambition. Like many school superintendents in Mississippi, the River City superintendent is a former football coach. But he regards his job as a plum won after many thumb thrusts. He is anxious to succeed to greater heights, and success, in his field, can be reflected from advantages gained by the money pried out of Washington. The River City school headquarters is a factory for the manufacture of federal grant proposals—over a million dollars worth for one school year. As the assistant superintendent put it, "We are out to get every dime Washington has to offer, and we're not going to let segregation stand in the way."

Unlike larger school systems, both Northern and Southern, the River City school people are new to the federal game and play it straight. They do not take money and at the same time seek to circumvent the spirit of civil rights legislation. They know they are being watched, and a detected mistake could be disastrous. Moreover, the bureaucracy is small enough to maintain control in the interests of efficiency. Thus, the superintendent and his assistant are inclined to favor faculty integration, because of the shortage of white teachers; they are also privately willing to replace

the inefficient "freedom of choice" system with neighborhood schools, even though this means sending white students to formerly all-Negro schools—a recognized danger
point.

All this is in sharp contrast with Bayou County. Meet
Mr. Sullivan, a high school principal in Raeford who has
been in his job 11 years. He says this is "too damn long,"
but then why hasn't he moved on and up? It seems he has
grown used to his comfortable salary and free house and
to appeasing the town's resident ideologists, a course which
has sealed him off from more sophisticated school districts,
such as River City. Listen to his statements:

> You get into a little place and you take the path of
> least resistance. That means you can never get out. . . .
> We small town officials are lonely men. I think my posi-
> tion is very similar to the President's. We often walk
> alone. . . . Occasionally I have to reassure them [the
> local extreme segregationists] by saying "Down with
> the niggers." . . . But I try to think of myself as more
> progressive and besides, as an administrator, I have a
> responsibility to everyone in my district.

All this suggests the plight of the Southern moderate
under duress. But we learned that Sullivan is the single
most despised white among Raeford Negroes and that he
rules the Negro schools with an iron hand while offering
rationalized clichés about the inferiority of Negro genes.
This is a man for whom the "path of least resistance" has
become a superhighway, one who fans local prejudices
instead of dissipating them. Unlike River City's administrators, he is an impediment, rather than a lubricant, in
the desegregation process. But also unlike the protected
bureaucrats in the larger towns, he stands naked before
a whirlwind of conflicting forces. Unhappily, his position
is typical in this region. River City may point the way to

the future. But most Delta communities are firmly mired in the past.

So far, however, we have neglected the Negro school administrators. Perhaps they belong in the consideration of the Negro community. But no. These men are cogs in the white machine, picked for docility. The "dual" system of education is a misnomer. There is only one, run by the whites, and Negro principals owe their very jobs to segregation. If faculties are desegregated, they will be the first to go. Not wishing to antagonize whites or Negroes, they opt out altogether. They don't tell their students to switch to white schools, and they don't tell them to stay away. They alone among school professionals continue to equivocate over the inferiority of Negro schools. None of this should be taken as denigration of individuals. Rather, it is one more instance of a social structure that resembles an increasingly heated griddle upon which men are reduced to batter.

It is a measure of the Negroes' tragedy that so much of this analysis should concern whites and thus indicate that the Negroes themselves have had relatively little voice in their ultimate destiny. But this is less true in River City than in Bayou County. What is there about the River City Negro community that has allowed it to play a more decisive role in determining its educational fate?

One crucial factor is the River City *black bourgeoisie*. True, the stereotype pictures the Negro middle class as the traditional lair of the "Uncle Tom," but, like all stereotypes, this one is dangerous. Some are "Toms," some are not. It depends on a complex set of factors such as vulnerability to reprisals, age, and relative position on the local political spectrum. River City has several middle class Negroes who are young, who are not vulnerable to white pressure in their occupation, whose images have become "whitened" in comparison to more radical civil rights workers. Such Negroes are hardly radicals themselves but neither have they turned their backs on the "movement." Taking advantage of their image as moderates, they push harder behind the scenes than the whites suspect. Not only do they provide examples by actually sending their own children to white schools (unlike middle class Negroes in most areas), but they also maintain a constant pressure on the white community that is felt despite its quiet subtlety. Using the need for federal funds as leverage, they have kept an eye peeled for violations of the desegregation requirements which might interest Washington. As one of them put it:

> We convinced Jones we would either make him or break him as superintendent. During the last six months he has undergone a fairly dramatic transformation for a white Southerner.

The present strategy of the River City Negro leaders is to engineer such an influx of Negro students into the white schools that, to relieve overcrowding, "freedom of choice" will have to be abandoned in favor of desegregation by neighborhoods. They reason that when white children are sent to a currently all-Negro school, greater attention will be given to facilities and educational standards.

The implementation of this strategy involves, among other things, the local Head Start program. In the summer of 1965 the only Head Start program in River City, serving mainly Negro children, was run by an outside agency— the Child Development Group of Mississippi—using civil rights workers. The city soon countered by setting up its own integrated Head Start board of directors, with a prominent Negro as president. To many whites, the Negro seemed "safe." On the contrary, he plans to take advantage of the trust to "funnel all of these Negro pre-schoolers right into the white first grades."

The point is not that the River City Negro *bourgeoisie* will move at an optimum pace or even that they would have begun at all without the outside civil rights workers forging the way and providing meaningful comparison. The point is rather that local Negro leaders and outside workers have provided a crucial alliance that may be as salutary in its results as it is uneasy in its day-to-day relations.

In Bayou County, however, the outside workers have had the reverse effect. There local whites and Negroes are farther apart than ever, since there are few middle class Negroes either informed or aggressive enough to take advantage of the situation and consolidate gains by coping with the whites from "inside." One or two urged poorer parents to send their children to white schools, but then failed to provide promised transportation or protection and, more importantly, failed to send their own children. Little wonder that only 2 percent of the Bayou County Negroes made the switch. Little wonder too that Bayou County whites are less impeded in planning for the future and are able to use subservient Negroes as window dressing. We have already mentioned the potential importance of Project Head Start in River City. The comparable program in Bayou County also has an integrated board of directors, but as one frustrated militant Negro leader said:

> The Negroes on the Board don't represent us. They were hand-picked to represent the whites. It looks like they're a lot of them, but the point is who are they?

To sum up, serious trouble has not yet occurred in Bayou County, but neither has serious integration. In so unpromising an atmosphere, violence is an ever looming threat, and the local Negroes lack the leadership to either curb the threat or act in spite of it. Again, this is less a failure of nerve than an artifact of community structure.

This report offers glimpses of optimism against a panorama of pessimism. Desegregation has gone a little farther and a little more smoothly in River City than in Bayou County. But in both places token compliance has been the rule. The point is not flagrant dereliction or defiance. The Office of Education has not cut off federal funds, even though both faculty and extracurricular activities should already have been desegregated under its formal requirements. Certainly federal pressure is increasing. But as yet there is no indication that pressure will be applied to force a shift from a "freedom of choice" system to a geographical basis of school attendance. Such a shift is too crucial to be left to local initiative. While it may occur in River City, it is unlikely in the near future of Bayou County.

And yet even geographical desegregation is no educational panacea. It may go beyond tokenism in racial matters since the "rednecks" who now live close to Negroes cannot afford to simply pack up their children and move to middle class white enclaves. But desegregation of this sort courts violence and ultimately differential education on the basis of social class if not race itself. The Negroes may find that a school in a poor neighborhood is never the greatest, whether black, white, or mixed.

This points again to the pervasive problem of poverty. On purely racial grounds, it may be that River City, Mississippi, will be more desegregated in 15 years than New York, Chicago, or Los Angeles—the impacted ghettos to which so many Mississippi Negroes have fled. But desegregation, educational or otherwise, can become a mockery to people so hopelessly poor. In the Delta, and throughout Mississippi, equal opportunity in any field means increasingly the opportunity to share *problems* rather than *benefits*. Equal schooling will continue to be poor

schooling. Equal employment may become equal vulnerability to unemployment, and equal voting only the chance
to make decisions of little impact.

There are immediate problems that can and must be
solved quickly with massive federal funds and stubbornly
executed federal legislation. But the tragedies of Mississippi have yet to reach their climax.

Postscript

The data and observations in this study go back more than a
year, but we have obtained more recent data on River City
and its school integration as of February 1967.

Little has changed in qualitative terms. Although a great
deal of flak was raised over the Office of Education guidelines
for the 1966-1967 academic year, the pattern of quiet compliance has remained as before. Because the number of classes to
be integrated through freedom of choice has doubled, so the
number of Negro students attending formerly all-white schools
has also doubled—but little more. Although the system has
yet to integrate the teaching staff, it is not alone in failing to
comply in this respect, and it has made a token response by
bringing the Negro administrator in charge of the Negro
schools into the offices of the white school administration.

But one ironic twist merits special attention. The River
City school system was successful in applying for federal free
lunch funds for schools with a high proportion of lower
class children, funds provided under the terms of the Elementary and Secondary Education Act. It now happens that
these "liberal" monies have unintentionally "conservative"
consequences: only the Negro schools had sufficient propor-
tions of lower class students to qualify. So if a Negro student
moves to a white school he loses his free lunch, sometimes
his only decent meal of the day. Here is yet another respect in
which integration involves a sacrifice rather than an unmixed
blessing. For many the hunger for food is understandably
more salient than the thirst for knowledge. Once again freedom of choice in the Delta offers a poor choice at best.

April 1967

FURTHER READING SUGGESTED BY THE AUTHORS:

Equality of Educational Opportunity by James S. Coleman, *et al.*
(Washington, D.C.: US Government Printing Office,
1966). A mammoth survey of the extent and consequences of
current segregation in which "separate" is shown to be
blatantly "unequal" despite the amount of money invested in
physical plants, teacher up-grading, etc.

The Negro American edited by Talcott Parsons
and Kenneth B. Clark (Boston: Houghton Mifflin Company,
1966). See "It's the Same, But It's Different" by Robert
Coles, a sensitive psychological portrait of the difficulties faced by
integrated Negro children.

Pickets at the Gates by Estelle Fuchs (New York: The
Free Press, 1966). A study of demonstrations in support of New
York school desegregation and the reactions elicited.

The Disadvantaged Learner edited by Staten Webster (San
Francisco: Chandler Publishing Company, 1966). An imposing
collection of essays by social scientists of all stripes on
research on the disadvantaged learner.

The Census Search for Missing Parents

ARLYNE I. POZNER

On a hot afternoon in the spring of 1960, 60-year-old Edna Williams answered a knock at the door of her frame house in rural Mississippi. She found a white woman with a large pad standing on the weather-scarred boards of the front porch. "I'm taking the census," the woman explained. "I'd like to ask you a few questions."

How many people lived at the Williams' house? Just the three of them, Mrs. Williams answered—herself, her husband Earl, and their eight-year-old granddaughter Phyllis. If the next seemingly logical question had been asked— what about Phyllis' parents? The answer would have been: "Gone to Chicago. Six, seven years ago. We're Phyllis' folks now. She's just like our own. She was born right here in this house, and she's been with us ever since."

But the question as to the whereabouts of Phyllis' real parents was not asked. It was not on the census forms that year. If it had been, things would have been much easier for the Justice Department when a complex case of racial discrimination erupted in Mississippi six years later, in the fall of 1965.

In the summer of 1965, the Mississippi state legislature passed a law stipulating that children whose parents lived *out of state* would be required to pay up to $350 per year tuition to attend the public schools. Children who would not or could not pay the tuition would simply be excluded from classes.

Mississippi is one of only three states where such a law could have been passed. (Virginia and South Carolina are the others.) All the other states have compulsory school attendance laws which require school-age children to attend classes, thus they automatically bar any legislation that would interfere with this principle of universal public education. (Mississippi, Virginia, and South Carolina have repealed their compulsory attendance laws. Alabama, Arkansas, Georgia, Louisiana, and North Carolina have provisions for waiving compulsory attendance for various reasons—riots, disasters, or "co-mingling of the races.") Mississippi was able to pass a law which read (in part):

No child . . . shall be included in the average daily attendance figures of any public school in the State of Mississippi . . . whose parent or parents, natural or adopted, or whose legally appointed guardian . . . is not an actual physical resident of the State of Mississippi, unless said child or person is residing in a recognized orphan or children's home, as distinguished from a foster home; or unless the parents . . . are presently serving outside the State of Mississippi, on active duty in the Armed Forces of the United States; or unless said child shall pay or there shall be paid on its behalf, such tuition fee . . . which shall be at least commensurate with the average cost of education per pupil in the school district.

Who stood to be penalized by this law? Children like the Williams' granddaughter Phyllis. Her real parents had left Mississippi for Chicago. The Williamses were not her natural or legally adopted parents, nor could they afford to pay several hundred dollars a year to keep their granddaughter in school. When the new term started in September, she and other "parentless" children were turned away from the schools that many of them had been attending for years. It soon became apparent that most of the children turned away were Negro. Within a few weeks, the NAACP Legal Defense and Education Fund in Jackson had received numerous complaints from concerned "nonparents."

The discriminatory effect of the bill was underlined by another law, passed in the same legislative session, which provided state funds to pay the tuition of students attending nondenominational *private* schools. The only accredited schools in Mississippi that answered this description were all white. (The state's two nondenominational private Negro schools were not recognized by the State Board of Education.) As the *Jackson Clarion-Ledger* quite forthrightly summed it up on September 9, 1965: "The system was adopted during the recent term of the legislature as an aid in the establishment of segregated white schools in Mississippi." It added, "A number of schools have been established—three in Jackson and one in Clarksdale."

Mississippi was, in effect, challenging the federal government on two fronts—by the effort to use state funds to set up a segregated "private" school system for whites only, and by the effort to exclude Negro children with neither parents nor money from the public schools. The latter situation was particularly urgent and demanded immediate action, because children were losing valuable school days.

The NAACP lawyers in Jackson started prompt litigation against the bill, and the Justice Department quickly inter-

TABLE 1—SCHOOL-AGE CHILDREN IN MISSISSIPPI, 1960

All persons 5-18 years old	Negro	(%)	White	(%)	Total	(%)
Total (excludes other nonwhite)	316,892	(49.4)	324,243	(50.6)	641,135	(100.0)
Living with neither parent	43,397	(82.1)	9,459	(17.9)	52,856	(100.0)
Living with at least one parent	273,495	(46.5)	314,784	(53.5)	588,279	(100.0)

vened in their behalf. At this point the Bureau of the Census, not normally involved in implementing public policy, was drawn into the case. Attorney General Nicholas Katzenbach needed certain figures. How many children like Phyllis were there in the state of Mississippi—children whose real parents lived outside the state and whose "nonparents" could not, for legal or financial reasons, adopt them of pay tuition? More important, what percentage of them were Negro? The bias in the tuition law seemed obvious, but without figures to firmly establish that Negro children were substantially harder hit by the law than whites, the government's case would be difficult to prove.

There were no simple answers available. The immediate and major problem was that the routine questions asked on the census form pertained only to the characteristics of persons living together in the same home. This automatically excluded any direct information about parents who were not living with their children. Whether the parents of these "parentless" children were living in a neighboring state, in a neighboring town, in the same town, or even next door could not be ascertained from the census figures alone. So there was no direct way to know how many children's parents lived out of state, much less what percentage of these children were Negro.

This left the Justice Department in an awkward situation. Publications or tabulations of the Bureau of Census, if placed under the Census seal, constitute legitimate evidence in a court of law. But other demographic interpretations, in contrast, cannot stand alone as legal evidence; they must be presented by a demographer acting as an expert witness.

Furthermore, census figures, though admissible as legal evidence, are sometimes inaccurate. For example, it has been estimated that at least 15 percent of the young, nonwhite

TABLE 2—INCOME AND HOUSEHOLD SIZE, 1960

	Negro		White	
Number of households				
All households	128,232	(100.0%)	207,915	(100.0%)
Households with at least one "parentless" child	35,992	(28.1%)	10,712	(5.2%)
Households with all children living with at least one parent	92,240	(71.9%)	197,203	(94.8%)
Average size of household (persons)				
All households	6.0		4.5	
Households with at least one "parentless" child	5.8		4.5	
Households with all children living with at least one parent	6.1		4.5	
Income of household (median)				
All households	$1569		$4675	
Households with at least one "parentless" child	1429		3365	
Households with all children living with at least one parent	1623		4731	

men living in large metropolitan areas like Chicago and Detroit were missed in the 1960 census. They simply "vanished" and were invisible to the census enumerator, likely due to frequent changes of residence.

Nevertheless, the Justice Department must work within the law; and in the Mississippi tuition case, the law had to move quickly to keep children from missing valuable education time.

Lacking direct information, Justice Department lawyers relied on a retabulation of 1960 census records to describe a special population of children not living with either parent. Thus any Negro-white differences in this special population would have to be extended to the target group— children whose parents no longer lived in Mississippi—by the lawyer's arguments.

Tables 1 and 2 summarize the key characteristics of Mississippi children not living with either parent. Striking, though not unanticipated, was the finding that 82 percent of these children were Negro. Less than 3 percent of all white children of school age lived with neither parent, but fully 14 percent of Mississippi's school-age Negro children fell into this category.

The average Negro household containing at least one "parentless" child houses 5.8 persons and has an annual income of $1,429. This allows less than $250 annually per person. To pay tuition for just one child ($350) eats up more than one person's yearly allotment. Also, since one-third of these households are very large (seven or more people), it is possible that they will contain more than one "parentless" child.

The situation is quite different for the average white household which might be subject to tuition charges. This average household contains 4.5 persons and reports an annual income of $3,365, or $750 per person per year.

Obviously, it is less of a sacrifice for the average white household to pay the prescribed tuition charges than for the average Negro household.

The next step was clear. The crucial point for the Justice Department lawyers to prove was that the parents of the "parentless" Negro children were, in fact, living outside the state of Mississippi, for it was only on this condition that the children could be excluded from school.

The best evidence available for this purpose was, again, furnished by the Bureau of the Census. The focus this time was on "state of birth" information. By ascertaining what proportion of the Negroes born in Mississippi still lived there, the lawyers could obtain a rough picture of Negro outmigration—outmigration which presumably included the parents of "parentless" children left in Mississippi.

From 1950 "state of birth" figures, demographer Everett Lee showed that throughout the nation 29 percent of non-whites lived outside their state of birth as compared with 25 percent of whites. But, he pointed out, at the youngest ages, relatively fewer, and in the middle ages many more, nonwhites had left the state of birth. He went on to conclude that "an important factor in the low proportion of interstate migrants among young nonwhite children is the ancient custom of Southern Negroes of leaving the children with the mother or grandmother while the father or parents go away in search of economic opportunity."

In 1960 the pattern was similar. Twenty-nine percent of nonwhites in the United States and 27 percent of whites lived outside their state of birth. More pronounced differences show up when the state of birth is Mississippi.

A larger proportion of nonwhites born in Mississippi left the state during their lifetimes (up to 1960) than did whites. As in Lee's 1950 figures, the only exceptions were the younger age groups. The fact that the white outmigration is higher among young groups, while lower in all others, may indeed suggest that nonwhite children are left behind more frequently than white children.

Other sources confirm this. Morton Rubin reports:

Approximately one-third of the migrants were single at the time of first migration. Another third were married and had children, but wives sometimes migrated later, and children very frequently were left with relatives while parents migrated. Respondents felt that children complicated migration, prohibiting it or at least delaying it. Migration by individuals was sometimes a consequence of separation, and destinations were often chosen with a view of making distance from partner a release from alimony or other obligations.

Eric Krystall found the same pattern true of some Negro migrants in Detroit.

The Mississippi state census report offers further evidence that Negro parents often leave their children behind with relatives when they migrate north in search of better jobs and higher pay. The ratio of children to family heads among Negroes in Mississippi is 2.14 children per family head. In Chicago—a prime target of Negro migration from Mississippi—the figure is only .77 children per head. This also suggests when they migrate to Northern cities, Negro parents do not take their children. However, as has been mentioned, all of this is interpretive evidence. It is not, in and of itself, admissible as legal evidence. It needs an expert witness to do the interpreting before the judge.

For reasons not entirely clear, possibly as a result of the Attorney General's case, the state of Mississippi backed down in the last week of April, and repealed the tuition bill. After months of litigation, the state legislature rescinded Senate Bill 1516. It issued no official statement as to why.

The tuition bill case in Mississippi is not the first state

attack upon the Supreme Court decision of 1954, and it is surely not the last. But there is a new element in the federal government's counterattacks as it mobilizes previously uninvolved departments in the attempt to bring the recalcitrant Southern states into compliance with national policies.

Already the Justice Department has called on the Bureau of the Census for evidence in other cases of allegedly discriminatory state laws in the South. Census figures were used to challenge Mississippi's poll tax law, and a similar case is pending in Alabama.

Undoubtedly, other legal uses of census statistics will be developed as government lawyers learn the power of such information.

January/February 1967

How
Southern Children Felt
About King's Death

JAMES W. CLARKE/JOHN W. SOULE

Shortly after Martin Luther King's death on April 4, 1968 we set forth to investigate how Negro and white children had reacted to the assassination. Our inquiry was conducted along lines similar to those charted by social scientists who had studied children's reactions to the assassination of John F. Kennedy.

There were parallels between King's death and the death of John F. Kennedy in 1963—and the more recent death of Robert F. Kennedy in June, 1968. In each case, a relatively young public leader was cut down during his prime years. All of these men had been associated with the civil rights movement—King, the movement's spiritual leader; the two Kennedys, political leaders closely identified with and sympathetic to the cause of Negro equality.

The association between the three leaders began during the 1960 Presidential campaign when the Kennedys intervened after King had been jailed for his civil rights activities in Atlanta, Ga. (King had been sentenced to four months' hard labor and was being held on a legal technicality. The Kennedy brothers telephoned to remonstrate with the judge who had sentenced King. King was released from jail the following day.) The ties between them remained close until the assassinations. All three men were also unpopular with those who objected to the civil rights movement.

Our study was designed to answer four questions:

■ How did schoolchildren react—intellectually and emotionally—to King's death?

■ Were their responses similar to those reported among children after President Kennedy's assassination?

■ Were there differences between the reactions of white children and Negro children? and

■ What effect did their parents' attitudes—as perceived by the children—have upon their own reactions?

Clearly, children are not exempt from political attachments; in fact, it is during childhood that people develop their most enduring values and preferences. Indeed, as the recent civil disorders show, young people may even become political actors of the first order—in Detroit, for example, 61.3 percent of the rioters were between 15 and 23 years of age. In China, teenagers were prominent in the recent Cultural Revolution.

Our subjects were students attending four public schools in two metropolitan communities in north and southeast Florida. They included 165 whites and 217 Negroes from seventh-, ninth-, and eleventh-grade classes. Except for the eleventh-graders, all were attending schools that were essentially segregated.

In each class, the regular teacher distributed and administered our questionnaires. We, as two white university-professors, avoided any contact with the students in order to prevent any bias that might have been introduced by our presence. Every effort was made to keep from disrupting the normal classroom situation. And in selecting the sample, we tried to include a comparable number of Negro and of white students within each grade level.

Why were the sampling techniques not more rigorous? Simply because of time: We wanted to complete the survey as soon after the assassination as possible. As it was, the data were collected within 12 days after the assassination. This delay was caused by our having had to obtain the approval of school officials.

The data in Table 1 show a clear difference between the races in their reactions to King's assassination: Whites were distinctly less distressed than Negroes.

REACTIONS BY RACE TO KING'S ASSASSINATION		(Table 1)
Initial Reactions	Negroes (Number: 189)	Whites (Number: 141)
Shocked, grieved, saddened, or angry	96%	41%
Indifferent or pleased	4	59
	100%	100%

The responses were elicited by asking students the open-ended question, "How did you feel when you first heard of Dr. King's death?" Only two of the 382 respondents could not identify King. Fifty-two students answered "don't know" or "no response." (In investigating students' attitudes, particularly those of young students, a substantial number of "no reponses" is to be expected.) Of those who did answer, reactions varied from a deep sense of sorrow to feelings of elation. Fifty-nine percent of the white students were indifferent or elated. Ninety-six percent of the Negro students expressed shock or grief.

REACTIONS OF WHITES BY SEX TO KING'S ASSASSINATION		(Table 2)
Initial Reactions	Males (Number: 70)	Females (Number: 71)
Shocked, grieved, saddened, or angry	27%	55%
Indifferent or pleased	73	45
	100%	100%

What role, if any, did the sex of the respondents play in answering this question? Table 2 shows that white boys were appreciably less upset about King's assassination than white girls. Seventy-three percent of the white boys expressed either indifference or satisfaction—compared with 45 percent of the white girls. Virtually no difference was found between the reactions of Negro boys and girls.

That parents transmit their attitudes and values to their children has been well documented. With regard to King's assassination, we found a close correspondence between parents' responses (as perceived by the students) and the students' own responses. (See Table 3.)

Previous research has also repeatedly shown a link between racial prejudice and class—for example, more lower-status whites tend to be prejudiced than high-status whites.

PERCEIVED PARENTS' REACTIONS & (Table 3)
CHILDREN'S REACTIONS

Children's Reactions	Perceived Parents' Reactions	
	Felt Bad (Number: 111)	Indifferent or glad (Number: 80)
Felt Bad	97%	17%
Indifferent or glad	3	83
	100%	100%

Note: Fully 50% of the sample were unable or unwilling to report their perceptions of their parents' attitudes.

Our findings confirm this. (See Table 4.) Indifference and pleasure after King's death were found among significantly more white students whose fathers were in clerical, sales, and laboring occupations (82 percent) than among white students whose fathers were in professional, managerial, or official occupations (35 percent). Further, 65 percent of these higher-status children expressed sadness or sympathy.

FATHER'S STATUS & WHITE (Table 4)
STUDENTS' INITIAL REACTIONS

Students' Initial Reaction	Father's Occupation	
	Professional, Proprietors, Managers, Officials	Clerical, Sales, Laborers
	(Number: 65)	(Number: 51)
Shocked, grieved, saddened, or angry	65%	18%
Indifferent or pleased	35	82
	100%	100%

Additional evidence of class differences appears when the parents' race is considered, and their reactions to the assassination are tabulated with regard to occupation. Table 5, in conjunction with Table 4, shows that children evidently share the basic class biases of their parents. Sixty-three percent of the white children's fathers in lower-level occupations were either pleased by or indifferent about King's death—compared with 82 percent of their children. On the other hand, while it is hardly encouraging, fewer of the white children's parents in higher-level occupations shared these attitudes (25 percent of the parents, 35 percent of their children). The Negro students, however, were overwhelmingly saddened by the event without regard to class differences, as were their parents.

The students were also asked, "Did you say any special prayer or attend a memorial service for Dr. King?" Seventy percent of the Negroes said Yes, as opposed to only 17 percent of the whites. (Paul B. Sheatsley and Jacob J. Feldman reported that three-fourths of a national sample of adults answered Yes to a similar question after President Kennedy's assassination.)

The Negro students, we learned, attend church more regularly than whites do. Yet the students' record of church attendance in the past seemingly had little bearing on whether they prayed after King's assassination. Most Negroes did pray and most whites did not, regardless of their past record of attending church.

Another question was, "What do you think should happen to the person who shot Dr. King?" Sixty-five percent of the Negro students showed hostility toward the murderer or a desire for revenge (Table 6). Typical responses were:

PARENTS' REACTIONS TO THE ASSASSINATION & FATHER'S STATUS

Parents' Reactions	Professional, Managerial, etc.		Working-Class	
	Negroes (Number: 40)	Whites (Number: 65)	Negroes (Number: 101)	Whites (Number: 56)
Felt bad	73%	34%	73%	12%
Indifferent or pleased	2	25	2	63
Not sure	25	41	25	25
	100%	100%	100%	100%

HOW SHOULD KING'S KILLER BE TREATED?		(Table 6)
Proposed Treatment	Negroes (Number: 198)	Whites (Number: 151)
Tried, punished by courts, imprisoned	35%	65%
Killed	65	18
No punishment, congratulated	0	17
	100%	100%

Seventh-grade Negro—"He should be hanged by the neck on public TV."

Ninth-grade Negro—"He should be shot by Mrs. King or King's brother."

Eleventh-grade Negro—"He should be taken out and beaten. Why don't they set him loose on [a Negro university] campus? We would do the job on him, but good!"

Only 18 percent of the whites shared similar but less intense attitudes. Conversely, some 65 percent of the whites felt that the assassin should be accorded due process of law. But *17 percent of the white students felt that the killer should be set free—or congratulated.* Among such responses:

Seventh-grade white—"He should go free."

Ninth-grade white—"He should get the Congressional Medal of Honor for killing a nigger."

Eleventh-grade white—"We should try him in court and find him not guilty. He did what lots of us wanted to do; he had the guts."

Moreover, sympathy for the killer among whites increased with their grade level. Thus, about 30 percent of the white eleventh-graders wanted no punishment for the assassin, compared with only 4 percent of the white seventh-graders. As the grade level of the Negro children increased, however, they were much more likely to favor due process of law as opposed to extra-legal, violent, or revengeful punishments. While 74 percent of the seventh-grade Negroes wanted to deal violently with the assassin, only 50 percent of the eleventh-grade Negroes did. Still, it is noteworthy—and alarming—that at all grade levels a majority of the Negro students favored some form of violent death for the killer, with no mention of customary legal procedures.

WHO WAS TO BLAME FOR KING'S DEATH?		(Table 7)
Blame Placed Upon	Negroes (Number: 154)	Whites (Number: 138)
A white man	35%	12%
Killer's color not mentioned	34	30
King himself was to blame	4	41
A prejudiced, racist, sick society	27	17

The students were also asked, "Who or what do you think is to blame for his [King's] death?" The data in Table 7 indicate that 35 percent of the Negro students identified the assassin as a white man as opposed to 12 percent of the whites. Forty-one percent of the white students thought that King was to blame for his own death. Only 4 percent of Negroes felt this way. About 24 percent of all the students refused to speculate on who the assassin might be: 16 percent of the whites and 29 percent of the Negroes.

After President Kennedy's assassination, not one child—white or Negro—was reported as saying that "We are all to blame." Our findings are quite divergent. Some 27 percent of the Negroes blamed American society for King's death, as did 17 percent of the whites. But whereas whites tended to blame the ills of American society in general, the Negroes tended to blame specifically the racist character of American society.

OCCUPATIONAL STATUS & (Table 8)
ATTITUDE ON CIVIL RIGHTS MOVEMENT

Parents' Attitudes on Civil Rights	Managers, Proprietors, Officials		Sales, Clerical, Laborers	
	Negroes (Number: 107)	Whites (Number: 73)	Negroes (Number: 102)	Whites (Number: 59)
Favorable	50%	16%	54%	2%
Unfavorable	7	36	5	64
No Answer	43	48	41	34
	100%	100%	100%	100%

When we asked the children in our study how their parents felt about the civil rights movement, we made a surprising discovery: Many of the Negro students either did not know or gave no answer. (See Table 8.)

Forty-three percent of the Negroes whose parents were in high-status occupations fell into this category, as did 41 percent of the Negroes whose parents were in low-level occupations. Compared with white students of high-status parents, a somewhat greater number of Negro students of high-status parents were knowledgeable (43 percent versus 48 percent gave no answer). Compared with white students of low-status fathers, many more Negro students of low-status parents were less knowledgeable (41 percent verus 34 percent).

Since civil rights should be far more important to Negroes than to whites, these figures are somewhat surprising. Perhaps Negro parents fail to communicate their attitudes to their children: This may be a reflection of the apathy so commonly attributed to Southern Negroes. Or perhaps Southern Negro children are just afraid of admitting that their parents favor civil rights.

Just as we found that white parents in low-status occupations were less sympathetic to King's death than white parents in high-status occupations, we found essentially the same pattern with regard to the civil rights movement. (Table 8.) Among higher-status white parents, there was much more ambivalence toward the movement—or perhaps a greater reluctance on the part of their children to reveal their parents' attitudes on this issue.

We also discovered that there is a very high level of

CHILDREN'S & PARENTS' ATTITUDES (Table 9)
TOWARD THE CIVIL-RIGHTS MOVEMENT

Negro & White Children's Attitudes	Perceived Parents' Attitudes		
	Favorable (Number: 127)	Unfavorable (Number: 88)	Don't Know (Number: 160)
Favorable	79%	7%	26%
Unfavorable	6	73	24
Don't Know	15	20	50
	100%	100%	100%

agreement between the students' values regarding the civil rights movement and the values they view their parents as holding. (See Table 9.) When we exclude the sizable "don't know" responses, from our knowledge of perceived parents' attitudes we can predict the children's attitudes with 73 percent accuracy.

When we analyzed these results by the grade level of the students, we found that, as their grade level increased, Negroes were more likely to blame a racist society for King's death. Younger Negroes tended to view the event in a more limited perspective—to blame it on "a white man." Among the white students, as grade level increased, more of them put the blame on King himself. Over 66 percent of the white eleventh-graders blamed King for his own assassination.

Studies made after the assassination of President Kennedy also revealed that more Negroes, both adults and children, expressed sorrow over his death than whites—like the Negro students in our study in response to King's death. Some of the items used in the study of reactions to President Kennedy's death were included in our questionnaire. (See Table 10.)

By and large, whites responded more emotionally to President Kennedy's assassination than to King's. More "felt the loss of someone very close" (a 54 percent difference), more "felt so sorry for his wife and children" (a 31 percent difference), more "felt angry that anyone could do such a terrible thing" (a 34 percent difference), more "hoped that the man who shot him would be killed" (a 16 percent difference), more "felt ashamed that this could happen in this country" (a 23 percent difference), and more were "so confused and upset I didn't know what to feel" (a 29 percent difference). On the other hand, more whites were "worried what would happen to our country"

CHILDREN'S REACTIONS TO THE TWO ASSASSINATIONS (Table 10)

	This Is How I Felt			
	King Reactions		Kennedy Reactions*	
	Negroes (Number: 217)	Whites (Number: 165)	Negroes (Number: 342)	Whites (Number: 1,006)
Felt the loss of someone very close	89%	15%	81%	69%
Worried what would happen to our country	88	85	74	63
Felt so sorry for his wife and children	98	63	91	94
Felt angry that anyone should do such a terrible thing	95	47	84	81
Hoped the man who killed him would be shot	76**	20**	54	36
Felt ashamed that this could happen in my country	77	63	75	86
Was so confused and upset I didn't know what to feel	40	15	40	44
Felt in many ways it was (King's) (Kennedy's) own fault	10**	49**	18	15

* Data from Roberta S. Sigel.
** The differences between these responses and the responses presented in Tables 6 and 7 are explained by the fact that a larger number of students responded to the items that appear in this table.

after King died (a 22 percent difference); and more "felt in many ways it was King's own fault" (a 34 percent difference).

The feelings of Negroes after the two assassinations were similar—but after King's death more were "worried what would happen to our country" (a 14 percent difference) and more "hoped that the man who shot him would be killed" (a 22 percent difference).

To be sure, these findings, in general, could have been foreseen. It can be argued that Negroes, because of their tragic history in this country, are more smitten by the death of any leader who seemed to be sympathetic to the cause of human equality. And it certainly could have been expected that a greater number of Negroes would feel unhappiness at the death of a Negro leader than whites would—just as more Catholics probably felt unhappy about Cardinal Spellman's death than Protestants and Jews did, and more Jews probably felt unhappy about Rabbi Wise's death than Christians did. But what is significant here is the striking differences between whites and Negroes in their reactions to King's death: Only 15 percent of the white students "felt the loss of someone close"; 49 percent of the white students "felt in many ways it was King's fault" (compared with only 15 percent of them feeling that way about Kennedy's death); 59 percent of the white students, as we have seen, felt indifferent about or pleased by King's death; and 17 percent of them felt that King's assassin should be freed or congratulated.

Yet perhaps the most disturbing findings of our study are:
1. fifty-nine percent of the white students were indifferent or pleased that King had been killed;
2. among the white students, happiness about and indifference toward King's death increased with their grade level;

3. Negro students became more likely to blame a racist white society for King's death as their grade levels increased; and

4. over 50 percent of all Negro students expressed a desire for extralegal revenge on King's assassin.

These findings, while only suggestive, provide no basis for optimism in regard to race relations in the South.

October 1968

What Black Power Means to Negroes in Mississippi

JOYCE LADNER

For three months during the summer of last year, I conducted a study aimed at finding out how Mississippi Negroes who endorsed "black power" interpreted this new concept. I learned that even those civil-rights activists who welcomed the concept attached curiously different meanings to it. My research also helped me understand why the black-power slogan proved so welcome to these activists—and why its acceptance was accompanied by the expulsion of whites from positions of leadership. Finally, my investigation provided some hints on the usefulness of the black-power slogan in helping Mississippi Negroes achieve their goals.

The black-power concept that emerged during the past year created fierce controversy, not only among white liberals but among Negro activists and conservatives. Most of the nation's top civil-rights leaders denounced the slogan—or vigorously embraced it. Instead of "black power,"

Martin Luther King Jr. advocated the acquisition of "power for all people." The N.A.A.C.P.'s Roy Wilkins, in condemning the slogan, used such terms as "anti-white power . . . a reverse Hitler . . . a reverse Ku Klux Klan and . . . can only mean black death." On the other hand, Stokely Carmichael, former head of SNCC, was the chief advocate of the slogan, which he defined as "the ability of black people to politically get together and organize themselves so that they can speak from a position of strength rather than a position of weakness." CORE's Floyd McKissick agreed.

But though Negro civil-rights leaders were divided about black power, the slogan was welcomed by many disenchanted Negroes living in Northern ghettos. These Negroes tended to view black power as a tangible goal that, when acquired, would lift them from their inferior positions in the social structure. Still, despite the positive identification that Negroes in the Northern ghettos had with the rhetoric of black power, SNCC and CORE made no massive attempts to involve these Negroes in black-power programs.

But what about the South? How did Negroes in Mississippi, and civil-rights organizations in Mississippi, interpret the new slogan? This was what I wanted to find out.

I used two methods of study. The first was *participant-observation*—in informal, small meetings of civil-rights activists; in civil-rights rallies; and in protest demonstrations, including the historic Meredith march. The second was the *focused interview*. I chose to interview 30 Negroes who, I had found, were in favor of black power. All were friends or acquaintances of mine, and all had had long experience in Southern civil-rights work. They represented about two-thirds of the black-power leaders in the state. (My personal involvement with the civil-rights movement helped provide the rapport needed to acquire the observational data, as well as the interview data.)

Among other things, I learned that many Negro activists in Mississippi had immediately embraced the black-power slogan—because of the already widely-held belief that power *was* an effective tool for obtaining demands from the ruling elite in Mississippi. Since 1960, civil-rights organizations have been playing a major role in involving Mississippi Negroes in the fight for equality. As a result, these Negroes became more and more dissatisfied with their impoverished, powerless positions in the social structure. The 1960 census reports that the median family income for Mississippi Negroes (who constitute 42.3 percent of Mississippi's population) was $1168, as opposed to $3565 for whites. Until fewer than five years ago, only 6 percent of the eligible Negroes were registered to vote. Today, the traditional all-white primary still exists—in almost the same form as it did 25 years ago. Since many of the efforts Mississippi Negroes made to change the social structure— through integration—were futile, they began to reconceptualize their fight for equality from a different perspective, one designed to acquire long-sought goals through building bases of power.

The black-power concept was, then, successfully communicated to Mississippi Negroes because of the failure of integration. But it was also communicated to them by the shooting of James Meredith on his march through Mississippi. This act of violence made Negro activists feel justified in calling for "audacious black power." For only with black power, they contended, would black people be able to prevent events like the shooting.

But there were varying degrees of acceptance of the slogan among Mississippi Negroes. Some, of course, did not accept the slogan at all—those who were never part of the civil-rights movement. Despite the fact that Mississippi has been one of the centers of civil-rights activity in the United States for the past six or seven years, no more than half the Negro population (I would surmise) has ever been actively involved in the movement. In such areas as Sunflower County, a very high percentage of Negroes have participated; but in many other areas, like Laurel, only a small percentage of the Negroes have taken part.

As for those Negroes active in the movement, they can be broadly classified into two groups. The first: the traditional, moderate, N.A.A.C.P.-style activists, who boast of having been "freedom fighters" before the "new movement" came into existence. They include ministers; small-businessmen; professionals; a sizable following of middle-class people; and a small number of the rank and file. Frequently the white ruling elite calls these activists the "responsible" leaders. The primary activities of this group include selling N.A.A.C.P. memberships; initiating legal action against segregation and discriminatory practices; negotiating with the ruling elite; and conducting limited boycotts and voter-registration campaigns.

The second group of activists are the less economically advantaged. Although a small number were once members of the N.A.A.C.P., most of them joined the movement only since 1960. They are readily identified with such organizations as the Freedom Democratic Party, CORE, SNCC, the Delta Ministry, and the Southern Christian Leadership Conference. Members of this group include plantation workers, students, the average lower-class Negro, and a small number of ministers, professionals, and businessmen. More militant than the first group, these activists conduct mass marches, large-scale boycotts, sit-ins, dramatic voter-registration campaigns, and so forth.

Members of the traditional organizations, in sum, are

still committed to working for integration. It is the militants who are oriented toward a black-power ideology, who consider integration irrelevant to what they see as the major task at hand—uniting black people to build black institutions. I suspect that a larger number of activists identify with traditional organizations like the N.A.A.C.P. than with the more militant ones.

The 30 black-power advocates I interviewed were, of course, the militant activists. Even so, I found that even these 30 could be further classified—into categories that Robert K. Merton has called *local* and *cosmopolitan*:

> The localite largely confines his interest to this [town of Rovere] community. Devoting little thought or energy to the Great Society he is preoccupied with local problems, to the virtual exclusion of the national and international scene. He is, strictly speaking, parochial.

> Contrariwise with the cosmopolitan type. He has some interest in Rovere and must of course maintain a minimum of relations within the community since he, too, exerts influence there. But he is also oriented significantly to the world outside Rovere and regards himself as an integral part of that world. . . . The cosmopolitan is ecumenical.

In this paper, I shall use "local" to refer to those long-term residents of Mississippi—usually uneducated, unskilled adults—whose strong commitment to civil-rights activity stemmed primarily from their desire to produce massive changes in the "home-front," the area they call home.

I shall use "cosmopolitan" to refer to the urbane, educated, highly skilled young civil-rights activists who are usually newcomers to Mississippi. Because they went to the state to work in the civil-rights movement only temporarily, their identification with the area tends to be weak.

One-third of my respondents, I found, hold the cosmopolitan view. The majority are Negro men, but there are a small group of Negro women and a very small group of white sympathizers. The mean age is about 23 or 24. About half are from the North; the remainder are from Mississippi and other Southern states. Most of the cosmopolitans are formally educated and many have come from middle-class Northern families and gone to the better universities. They are widely read and widely traveled. They are also artistic: Writers, painters, photographers, musicians, and the like are often found in the cosmopolitan group. Their general orientation toward life is an intellectual one. They are associated with SNCC, the Freedom Democratic Party, and CORE. Although a few are actively engaged in organizing black people in the various counties, much of their work in the state is centered on philosophical discussions, writing, and so forth. All of the cosmopolitans have had wide associations with white people. Some grew up and attended school with whites; other had contact with whites in the civil-rights movement. The cosmopolitans maintain that black people in American society must redefine the term "black" and all that it symbolizes, and that black pride and dignity must be implanted in all Negro Americans. The cosmopolitan position embraces the belief that the plight of Negro Americans is comparable to neocolonialized "colored peoples" of the world.

The cosmopolitans' participation in the Southern civil-rights scene, by and large, dates back to 1960 and the beginning of the student movement in the South. Their present ideology has to be viewed in the framework of the history of their involvement in the movement, with special emphasis on the negative experiences they encountered.

Some six years ago, black Americans began to seek their long-desired civil rights with a new sense of urgency. The N.A.A.C.P.'s painstaking effort to obtain legal, theoretical rights for Negroes was challenged. Groups of Negro college students in the South decided to fight the gradualism that had become traditional and to substitute radical action aimed at bringing about rapid social change. These students began their drive for equal rights with lunch-counter demonstrations. After much immediate success, they spread their drive to the political arena. Their only hope for the future, they felt, lay in the ballot. Much to their disappointment, acquiring political power was not so easy as integrating lunch counters. The students met their strongest resistance from whites in full possession of the sought-after political power. To deal with this resistance, the Federal Government passed two civil-rights laws: public accommodation and voting rights. But the Government did little to implement these laws. Still, in the early 1960s, student civil-rights workers had an almost unrelenting faith in the Federal Government and believed that changes in the laws would rapidly pave the way for sweeping changes in the social structure. This was the era when students were much involved in hard-core organizing. They paid little attention to abstract philosophizing. Instead they occupied themselves with such pressing problems as the mass arrests of Negroes in Greenwood, Miss.

As time went on, the cosmopolitans became more and more discouraged about their organizing efforts. They began to seriously question the feasibility of their strategies and tactics. By the end of 1964, after the historic Mississippi Summer Project, the cosmopolitans began to feel that their organizational methods were just not effective. For roughly a year and a half, they groped and searched for more effective strategies. Frequently they felt frustrated; sometimes they despaired. A number of them returned to the North and got well-paying jobs or went to graduate and professional schools. Others were alienated from some of the basic values of American society. Some students developed a strong interest in Africa and began to look to various African states as possible havens. Still others, after deciding that they had accomplished all that was possible through organizations such as SNCC, associated themselves with radical leftist groups.

It was during the tail end of this six-year period that two position papers were written by the cosmopolitans. One was by a group that insisted that Negroes expel whites from leadership roles in civil-rights organizations, and that Negroes develop "black consciousness" and "black nationalism." "Black consciousness" refers to a set of ideas and behavior patterns affirming the beauty of blackness and dispelling any negative images that black people may have incorporated about blackness. "Black nationalism" is a kind of patriotic devotion to the development of the Negro's own political, economic, and social institutions. Black nationalism is *not* a racist ideology with separatist overtones, however, but simply a move toward independence from the dominant group, the whites. This paper states:

> If we are to proceed toward true liberation, we must cut ourselves off from white people. We must form our own institutions, credit unions, co-ops, political parties, write our own histories. . . . SNCC, by allowing whites to remain in the organization, can have its efforts subverted. . . . Indigenous leadership cannot be built with whites in the positions they now hold. They [whites] can participate on a voluntary basis . . . but in no way can they participate on a policy-making level.

In response, one white civil-rights worker—Pat McGauley—wrote a paper acceding to the demands of the black-consciousness group:

> The time has indeed come for blacks and whites in the movement to separate; however, it must always be

kept in mind that the final goal of the revolution we are all working for is a multi-racial society.

The cosmopolitans I interviewed conceived of black power in highly philosophical terms—as an ideology that would unite black people as never before. To most of them, black power was intricately bound up with black consciousness. To a long-time SNCC worker, black consciousness was:

. . . an awareness of oneself as a removed nation of black people who are capable of running and developing their own governments and who have pride in their blackness to the extent that they won't sell out. . . . To the extent that he can say, "I'm no longer ashamed of my blackness." The individual redefines the society's rules in terms of his own being. There is a new kind of awakening of the individual, a new kind of realization of self, a type of security, and a type of self-confidence.

Another cosmopolitan equated black consciousness with community loyalty:

Black consciousness is not the question but rather [the question is] from which community one comes from. If you know that, you can identify with black people anywhere in the world then. That is all that is necessary.

These young people firmly believe that even the term "black" has to be redefined. To one of them, "Black has never had any favorable expression in the English language." To another, "American society has characterized black as the symbol for strength, evil, potency and malignancy. . . . People are afraid of the night, of blackness."

Most cosmopolitans feel that black people must acquire black consciousness before they can successfully develop the tools and techniques for acquiring black power. As one of them put it:

Black consciousness is the developmental stage of

black power. Black power will be incomplete without
black consciousness. Black consciousness is basically the
search for identity; or working out one's own identity.
. . . There must be a long process of learning and un-
learning in between and a period of self-questing.

In short, by developing black consciousness, a Negro can
appreciate his blackness and thus develop a kind of community loyalty to other colored peoples of the world.

Most of the cosmopolitans felt that the redefinition of
blackness must take place in the black community *on the
black man's terms.* When such a redefinition has taken
place, black men who feel psychologically castrated because
of their blackness will be able to compete with whites as
psychological equals. ("Psychologically castrated" is a popular term among cosmopolitans, and refers to Negroes
whose beliefs and behavior have become so warped by
the values of white American society that they have come
to regard themselves as inferior.)

Cosmopolitans are familiar with the works of Marcus
Garvey, Malcolm X, Franz Fanon, Kwame Nkrumah, and
other revolutionary nationalists. Some can quote passages
from their works. To the cosmopolitans, Marcus Garvey
(1887–1940), who tried to instill racial pride in Negroes,
was a pioneer of black nationalism and black consciousness
in America. The greatest impact on the cosmopolitans,
however, comes from the contemporary Malcolm X, whose
philosophy—toward the latter period of his life—reflected
a revolutionary spirit and a total dissatisfaction with the
plight of Negroes in this country. One of the cosmopolitans
had this to say about Malcolm X:

Malcolm was very much together. . . . He was a man
who knew what he was doing and would have eventually
showed everyone what he was capable of doing. . . .
Malcolm had history behind him and was with the cat

on the block.

To another:

Malcolm X . . . was able to relate to people and to the press. The press is your right arm. . . . In order to be a real militant, you have to use the man [press] and that is what Malcolm did. They [the press] didn't create Malcolm. . . . The press was attuned to Malcolm. . . . Malcolm was not attuned to the press.

Some cosmopolitans call themselves students of Malcolm X and express the hope that another such leader will soon emerge.

Another symbolic leader is the late Algerian revolutionary, Franz Fanon, whose *The Wretched of the Earth* has become a veritable Bible to the cosmopolitans. Fanon tried to justify the use of violence by the oppressed against the oppressor, and to relate the neocolonialization of the black man in Algeria to the plight of colored peoples everywhere. Similarly, the cosmopolitans have great admiration for Stokely Carmichael, one of their associates, whose philosophy is highlighted in this passage:

The colonies of the United States—and this includes the black ghettos within its borders, north and south—must be liberated. For a century this nation has been like an octopus of exploitation, its tentacles stretching from Mississippi and Harlem to South America, the Middle East, southern Africa, and Vietnam; the form of exploitation varies from area to area but the essential result has been the same—a powerful few have been maintained and enriched at the expense of the poor and voiceless colored masses. This pattern must be broken. As its grip loosens here and there around the world, the hopes of black Americans become more realistic. For racism to die, a totally different America must be born.

Embodied within the philosophy of the cosmopolitans

is an essential proposition that American society is inherently racist, that the majority of white Americans harbor prejudice against black people. Few make any distinction between whites—for example, the white Southerner as opposed to the Northern liberal. Whites are considered symbolic of the black man's oppression, and therefore one should not differentiate between sympathetic whites and unsympathetic whites. The conclusion of the cosmopolitans is that any sweeping structural changes in American society can come about only through the black man's taking an aggressive role in organizing his political, economic, and social institutions. The black man must control his destiny.

I have categorized the remaining two-thirds of my 30 respondents as locals. (Of what significance these ratios are, by the way, I am not sure.) The locals are almost as committed to solving the pressing problems of inadequate income, education, housing, and second-class citizenship *practically* as the cosmopolitans are committed to solving them *philosophically*. Most of the locals are life-long residents of their communities or other Mississippi communities. Most of them, like the cosmopolitans, have been drawn into the movement only since 1960. Unlike the generally youthful cosmopolitans, the age range of the locals is from young adult to elderly. Many locals are indigenous leaders in their communities and in state-wide organizations. Whereas cosmopolitans tend to be middle-class, locals are members of the lower-class black communities and they range from plantation workers to a few who have acquired modest homes and a somewhat comfortable style of life. Many are leaders in the Mississippi Freedom Democratic Party, which in 1964 challenged the legality of the all-white Mississippi delegation to the national Democratic convention and in 1965 challenged the constitutionality of the elected white Representatives to serve in the U.S. House of Representatives. (Both challenges were based upon the fact that Negroes did not participate in the election of the delegates and Representatives.)

Although most of the locals are native Mississippians who have always been victimized by segregation and discrimination, I have also placed a number of middle-class students in this category—because of their very practical orientation to black power. The backgrounds of these students are somewhat similar to those of the cosmopolitans, except that the majority come from the South and are perhaps from lower-status families than the cosmopolitans are. These students are deeply involved in attempts to organize black-power programs.

Because of segregation and discrimination, the locals are largely uneducated; they subsist on a totally inadequate income; and they are denied the privileges of first-class citizenship. They have had a lot of experience with the usual forms of harassment and intimidation from local whites. Their entire existence can be perceived in terms of their constant groping for a better way of life. Because of many factors—like their low level of income and education and their Southern, rural, small-town mentality (which to some extent prevents one from acquiring an intellectualized world view)—the definition they have given to black power is a very practical one.

The black-power locals can be considered militants to much the same degree as the cosmopolitans, but on a different level. In essence, the nature and kind of activities in which they are willing to participate (voter registration, running for political office, boycotts, etc.) are indeed militant and are not surpassed by the nature and kind to which the cosmopolitans orient themselves. Indeed, in some cases the locals are deeply involved in realizing black-power programs: In certain counties, women have organized leathercraft and dress-making cooperatives. And in Senator Eastland's home county of Sunflower, an unsuccessful effort was even made to elect an all-black slate of public officials.

The great difference between cosmopolitans and locals is that the locals are committed to concrete economic and political programs, while the cosmopolitans—to varying degrees—endorse such programs but actually have made little effort to realize them.

Most locals perceived black power as a more effective, alternate method of organizing and acquiring those rights they had been seeking. In the past they had been committed to integration. Power had not originally been considered important in and of itself, for it was hoped that America would voluntary give Negroes civil rights. Therefore the locals sought coalition politics—they aligned themselves with Northern labor groups, liberals, national church groups, and so forth. During their several years of involvement, they—like the cosmopolitans—suffered many defeats. For example, many were involved with the Mississippi Summer Project, which brought hundreds of Northerners into the state in 1964. At that time the locals were convinced that such a program would bring about the wide structural changes they desired. But, to their disappointment, once the volunteers returned to the North the old patterns of segregation and discrimination returned. Some of the locals had gone to the Democratic Convention in Atlantic City, N.J., in 1964 hoping to unseat the all-white slate of delegates from Mississippi. When this failed, they invested further moral and physical resources into challenging the legality of the all-white slate of Mississippi Representatives in the U.S. House. Another set-back came when a large contingent pitched their tents on the White House lawn in a last-ditch effort to obtain poverty funds to aid in building adequate housing. All were sharecroppers, evicted because their participation in voter-registration programs was contrary to the desires of their plantation landlords. These evicted sharecroppers later set up residence in the buildings of the inactive Air Force base in Greenville, Miss. They were deeply depressed when officials of the Air Force ordered military police to remove them. One of the leaders of this group remarked, "If the United States Government cares so little about its citizens that it will not allow them to live in its abandoned buildings rather than in unheated tents [this occurred during winter], then that government can't be for real."

I submit that the events outlined above, among many others, caused a large number of the locals—like the cosmopolitans—to pause and question the effectiveness of their traditional organizational tactics and goals. Indeed, many even came to seriously question the Federal Government's sincerity about alleviating the problems of the Negro. A number of the participants in these events stopped being active in the movement. Others began to express strong anti-white sentiments.

Black power was embraced by many of the locals from the very beginning, and they began to reconceptualize their activities within the new framework. To the locals, black power was defined in various ways, some of which follow:

Voter registration is black power. Power is invested in the ballot and that's why the white man worked like hell to keep you away from it. . . . We were even taught that it was not right to register [to vote]. The civil-rights movement in this state started around the issue of voting—we shouldn't forget that.

Black power is political power held by Negroes. It means political control in places where they comprise a majority. . . . Black power is legitimate because any time people are in a majority, they should be able to decide what will and will not happen to them.

Black power was further viewed as a means of combining Negroes into a bond of solidarity. It was seen as a rallying cry, a symbol of identification, and a very concrete tool for action. Many said that former slogans and concepts such as "Freedom Now" were ambiguous. One could easily ask, "Freedom for what and from what?" One local said:

First we wanted Freedom Now. I ran around for six years trying to get my freedom. I really didn't know what it was.

Black power, they felt, was more concrete, for it had as its central thesis the acquisition of power. (Actually, the locals have also defined black power in various ways, and to some the slogan is as ambiguous as "Freedom Now.") The locals felt that Negroes would be able to acquire certain rights only through the control of their economic and political institutions, which—in some cases—also involves the eventual control of the black community. One black-power advocate put it succinctly when he said:

Black power means controlling the Negro community. It means that if the Negro community doesn't want white cops coming in, they can't come in. It means political, economic, and social control.

Asked how this control could be obtained, he replied:

We will have to start putting our money together to organize cooperatives, and other kinds of businesses. We can get political power by putting Negroes into public offices. . . . We will have to tell them to vote only for Negro candidates.

To others, control over the black community was not the goal, but rather a *share* in the existing power:

All we're saying to the white man is we want some power. Black power is just plain power. . . . It just means that Negroes are tired of being without power and want to share in it.

Thus, we can observe that there are several variations of the concept, all revolving around a central theme: the acquisition of power by Negroes for their own use, both offensively and defensively.

Despite the obvious practical orientation of the locals, there can also be found traces of black consciousness and black nationalism in their thought patterns. Most have never read Garvy, Fanon, Malcolm X, and other nationalists, but they tend to readily identify with the content of speeches made by Stokely Carmichael bearing the message of black nationalism. They are prone to agree with the cosmopolitans who speak to them about ridding themselves of their "oppressors." When the chairman of the Mississippi Freedom Democratic Party speaks of overthrowing neo-colonialism in Mississippi, shouts of "Amen!" can be heard from the audience. There is also a tendency in this group to oppose the current war in Vietnam on the grounds that America should first concentrate on liberating Negroes within the United States' borders. The locals also believe that the war is indeed an unjust one. Perhaps the following statement is typical:

Black men have been stripped of everything. If it takes plack power to do something about this, let us have it. Black power has got the country moving and white people don't like it. We marched into Dominica, we marched into Vietnam. Now if we [black people] can conquer this country, we will conquer the world.

There is a growing feeling among both locals and cosmopolitans of kinship with the colored peoples of the world, including the Vietnamese. To engage in warfare against other colored people is regarded as a contradiction of this bond of solidarity.

For both the Mississippi cosmopolitans and locals, then, it was mainly frustration that drew them to the concept of black power.

The black-power slogan should be viewed in the perspective of the overall civil-rights movement, one of the most popular social movements in the history of this country. Now, there are some scholars who maintain that, by viewing a particular social movement over a period of time, one can discern a typical sequence: the movement's crystallization of social unrest; its phase of active agitation and proselytism; its organized phase; and the achievement of its objectives. The civil-rights movement, with much success, achieved each of these phases—except the final one, the achievement of objectives. Despite the great amount of effort and resources expended by black people and their allies to obtain civil rights, there was a disproportionate lack of gains. Indeed, in much of Mississippi and the South, conditions have barely changed from 10 or even 20 years ago. Many black people are still earning their livelihood from sharecropping and tenant farming; many household heads are still unable to earn more than $500 a year; many black children are still deprived of adequate education because of the lack of facilities and adequately trained teachers. To date, only 42.1 percent of Negroes of voting age are registered as opposed to 78.9 percent of whites. We still hear of lynchings and other forms of violence of which Negroes are the victims.

The black-power thrust is thus an inevitable outgrowth of the disillusionment that black people have experienced in their intense efforts to become integrated into the mainstream of American society. Thwarted by traditional formulas and organizational restrictions, some Mississippi Negroes have responded to the black-power concept in a sometimes semirational, emotionally charged manner—because it seemed the only available resource with which they could confront white American society.

How was the black-power concept related to the expulsion of whites from leadership positions in the movement? The fact is that the alienation and disaffection found throughout the entire black-power group also resulted from strained interpersonal relations with white civil-rights workers. During the past two years, there has been a growing belief among black people in Mississippi that white civil-rights workers should go into the *white* communities of that state to work. Only then, they contended, could the "inherent racism" in American society, with particular reference to the "Southern racist," begin to be dealt with. Even the seriousness of white civil-rights workers was questioned. Many Negroes felt that a sizable number of them had come South mainly to resolve their very personal emotional difficulties, and not to help impoverished black Mississippians. Rather, they were considered rebellious youth who wanted only to act out their rebellion in the most unconventional ways. Stokely Carmichael stated:

> Too many young, middle-class Americans, like some sort of Pepsi generation, have wanted to come alive through the black community; they've wanted to be where the action was—and the action has been in the black community. . . .

> It's important to note that those white people who feel alienated from white society and run into the black society are incapable of confronting the white society with its racism where it really does exist.

Much strain also resulted from the inability of many black civil-rights activists—skilled organizers but lacking the formal education and other technical skills white workers possessed—to deal with the increased bureaucratization of the civil-rights movement (writing proposals for foundation grants, for example). Black activists, in addition, constantly complained about the focus of the mass media on white "all-American" volunteers who had come South to work in the movement. The media never paid attention to the thousands of black people who frequently took far greater risks. These factors played a major role in destroying the bond of solidarity that had once existed between whites and blacks in the movement. Before the emergence of the black-power concept, it is true, many young black civil-rights workers had cast white civil-rights workers in the same category as all other white people. The new slogan was, to some extent, a form of justification for their own prejudice against whites.

In terms of practical considerations, however, urging the white volunteers to leave the black communities has had negative effects. SNCC and CORE, which at one time directed most of the grass-roots organizing, have always depended upon the economic and volunteer resources of liberal white individuals and groups. These resources are scarce nowadays.

On another level, there have been positive results from removing whites from black communities. Black activists—all cosmopolitans and some locals—contend that, now that the whites have gone, they feel more self-confident and capable of running their own programs. They tend to view the earlier period of the movement, when whites played active roles in executing the programs, as having been a necessary phase; but they maintain that the time has arrived when black people must launch and execute their own programs.

Clearly, the long-range aims of the locals and cosmopolitans are basically the same. Unlike Negroes in such traditional organizations as the N.A.A.C.P., locals and cosmopolitans have turned away from integration. Both groups want to unite black people and build political, economic, and social institutions that will render a certain amount of control to the black community. For some time, however, the two groups have been operating on different levels. The cosmopolitans focus on developing black consciousness among black people, which they consider a necessary step to developing black power; the locals concentrate on solving the immediate problems resulting from segregation and discrimination.

While it may seem that the locals are more prudent and realistic than the cosmopolitans, it should be said that there are many positive features to black nationalism and black consciousness. It *is* important to establish a positive black identity in a great many sectors of the black communities, both North and South, rural and urban, lower and middle class. Indeed, it is both important and legitimate to teach black people (or any other ethnic minority) about their history, placing special emphasis upon the positive contributions of other black people. Thus black consciousness has the potential to create unity and solidarity among black people and to give them hope and self-confidence. Perhaps it fulfills certain needs in black people that society, on the whole, cannot. Martin Luther King has made the following statement about black consciousness:

> One must not overlook the positive value in calling the Negro to a new sense of manhood, to a deep feeling of racial pride and to an audacious appreciation of his heritage. The Negro must be grasped by a new realization of his dignity and worth. He must stand up amid a system that still oppresses him and develop an unassailable and majestic sense of his own value. *He must no longer be ashamed of being black.* (Emphasis mine.)

Moreover, the task of getting blacks to act *as blacks, by* themselves and *for* themselves, is necessary for developing black consciousness, or psychological equality. Thus one is led to the conclusion that black consciousness does *necessarily* call for the expulsion of whites from leadership roles in the black communities.

The locals, on the other hand, have adopted concrete strategies that, in reality, involve the same kind of techniques that existed in the integration era. Specifically, when they refer to developing black-power programs, they speak of registering to vote, running for political office, and building independent political parties. As for the economic situation, they have begun to concentrate on building cooperatives and small businesses, and on almost-exclusively patronizing black merchants in an effort to "keep the money in the black community." If we turn back two years, however, we find that the same strategies, though somewhat modified, were being used then. In the past, the locals concentrated on registering large numbers of black people to vote, in an effort to be able to have a voice in the decision-making apparatus. The emphasis is now on registering to vote so that the Negro can have control over his community and eventual control over his political destiny. Cooperatives were organized at least a year before the black-power concept emerged, but—ever since emphasis was put on economic control—there has been an expansion and intensification in certain sectors of this area. At present, cooperatives are still operating on a small-scale, though, considering the masses of people whose lives could be immensely improved by cooperatives.

The differences in the emphasis on priorities of achieving black power between locals and cosmopolitans can be viewed as complementary rather than oppositional, because each level of emphasis is vital for the achievement of their goals. This is becoming increasingly true since, within the last year, black-power advocates have taken a far more aggressive and militant stance toward the realization of such aims. Locals who a year ago might have questioned the importance and feasibility of "Black Liberation" schools, which teach black history and culture, are less likely to do so now. This is an indication that there is a trend toward unity between the groups. Because of the strong emphasis among some sectors of the black-power movement on drawing the parallels of the plight of black Americans with that of the inhabitants of the Third World, locals are quite likely to become more cosmopolitan through time.

Through the development of such unity, there is a great possibility that black-power advocates in Mississippi will again turn to creative, large-scale organizing that would incorporate the major emphases of each group: black consciousness and immediate gains.

The key question, of course, is, what are the prospects for Mississippi Negroes' developing black-power institutions in the near future? Clearly, this will depend to a great extent upon the number of organizers in the field, on adequate economic resources, and on commitments from major civil-rights organizations to the Mississippi scene. Certainly the presence of a local charismatic leader also would aid in the development of pervasive black-power institutions. Indeed, a black-power "prophet" whose task was to keep the message before all the advocates would give them immeasurable support and strength for their undertakings.

Where black-power institutions have a good chance of developing at present are in the small number of Mississippi counties where there are strong black-power organizations with large Negro voting populations. Since the cosmopolitans are reentering the field and beginning to organize (and some of the most skilled organizers are in this group), the prospects—here at least—seem favorable. On the other hand, it seems highly doubtful at this point that the needed resources can be obtained from the traditional sources (Northern students, white liberals, church and labor organizations). So these resources (inadequate as they may be) may have to be obtained from the black community. CORE and SNCC have already begun to establish financial bases in the black communities throughout the country. Should this tactic fail, perhaps there will be a revaluation of the strategies employed in the acquisition of black power.

November 1967

FURTHER READING SUGGESTED BY THE AUTHOR:

The Wretched of the Earth by Franz Fanon (New York: Grove Press, 1963). The role of violence in a revolutionary movement and the catharsis it gives the oppressed.

Where Do We Go From Here: Chaos or Community? by Martin Luther King (New York: Harper and Row, 1967). King analyzes past gains of the civil-rights movement and suggests further activities, all nonviolent.

Social Theory and Social Structure by Robert K. Merton (Glencoe, Ill.: The Free Press, 1963). See "Patterns of Influence: Locals and Cosmopolitans," an elaboration of the typologies used in this article.

White Reflections on Black Power by Charles E. Fager (Grand Rapids, Mich.: William B. Eerdmans Publishing Co., 1967). Fager argues that black people are justified in calling for black nationalism and black power. He suggests that white liberals continue to support the movement, but only when called upon, and that they withdraw from leadership roles to allow blacks to assert themselves as leaders.

Some Reservations
About Black Power

DAVID RIESMAN

My own experience with the Deep South has been
almost entirely vicarious, and my reflections on Joyce
Ladner's discerning observations are set forth in a spirit
of tentativeness and questioning.

The psychiatrist Robert J. Lifton, discussing the dissident
attitudes of young Japanese students, distinguishes two
non-accommodative attitudes, which he calls *Restorationist*
and *Transformationist.* The Restorationist looks back to
an earlier, more pastoral epoch and wants to radically re-
arrange and, if necessary, destroy contemporary society in
the name of the past. The Transformationist, on the other
hand, rejects the past as well as the present. Both styles
give their possessors a way of interpreting their despair
and frustration, as well as some sort of quasi-political,
quasi-mystical agenda to cope with these feelings. When
I was in Japan in 1961, I met some of the leaders of the
Zengakuren, the federation of Japanese students. With

their grandiose talk, they seemed much less pragmatic than comparable American student activists were at that time.

Today I am not so sure, because some American students, particularly whites who are devotees of black power, often remind me of the *Zengakuren*. Negro and white cosmopolitans in the civil-rights movement have a kind of nostalgia that leads them to believe that American society is now more corrupt, and perhaps even more racist, than it ever was. The war in Vietnam and white ethnic hostility in Cicero are viewed as part of an overall pattern so rotten and menacing that, as Fanon believed of the Algerian victims of colonialism, only violence by the oppressed can be therapeutic.

My own impression is somewhat different. It seems to me that conditions have changed considerably for the better during the last 10 or 20 years, even in the Deep South. The frustration and despair that Miss Ladner finds in the cosmopolitans seems to me essentially to reflect their disappointment that things are not getting better *fast* enough. This frustration and despair also seems to be the source of their assumption that American society and all whites are inherently racist, for this assumption protects them from ever again experiencing either illusion or betrayal. But this assumption is a simplification of life, and as a remedy for the ambiguities of existence I find it understandable but sad. Thus even Martin Luther King Jr. declares that his people feel American society "has become corrupt" and that the Establishment (whatever that is) is worse than it once was.

No doubt, for many Southern Negroes come North, the past *was* more secure and definitive: As they often say, you knew where you stood. For peasants forced out of sharecropper existence into urban ghettos, with no preparation for urban life, the present could in some sense be worse—more alive and free, but also more disorganized and threatening. For Northern Negro cosmopolitans come South, white violence and the omnipresent white hostility and condescension also provide a shock. It may well be that there *are* parts of the South where things have gotten absolutely, rather than relatively, worse. But, contrary to the cosmopolitan impression Miss Ladner accepts, and despite the deprivations, lynchings, and other violence, the relative opening-up of some aspects of Deep South life seems to me, as it does to many fearsome and threatened local whites, undeniable and almost certainly irreversible. This spring I read the local press and corresponded with students and faculty at a number of Southern Negro colleges where there have been demonstrations and protests. And I doubt if 10 or 20 years ago the students who boycotted classes at the State College in Orangeburg, S.C., would have been so certain that the white racists would not close the college down. Indeed, these students actually succeeded in ousting the college president—in a new squeeze between the considerably-more-tolerant white community and the much-less-tolerant Negroes.

This last example suggests a theme implicit in Miss Ladner's paper, namely, the elements of class as well as of racial hostility that are involved in some uses of the black-power concept. (I do not mean to suggest that class is more important than race, but only that it is largely covert and ancillary.) When the lower-class locals, or some of them, accept the ideological leadership of the migrating cosmopolitans, it has meant that the local, "established," middle-class Negro leadership has been ousted. The rejection of the whites, which Miss Ladner's paper describes, also has elements of class as well as racial conflict, since the whites are almost invariably from upper-class or upper-middle-class backgrounds.

However, if the whites are driven out physically, under the slogan of black power, does this mean that they are spiritually rejected also? We might ask whether girls in women's colleges think less about men than girls in coed colleges. The cosmopolitans at least have had contact with whites, and the white world inevitably presses its reminders on them. (The very fact that we whites talk constantly about black power, could, I am inclined to think, be felt by black-power advocates as an intrusion, as a mild kind of intellectual imperialism—hardly less so when ardent but nevertheless presently-excluded white fellow-travelers praise black power.) The locals, with far less personal experience and contact with whites, may—in the physical absence of the whites—become even shakier in their self-esteem, wavering between feelings of abasement and of grandiosity, outcomes that are all the more likely because, as Miss Ladner notes with great penetration, the slogan "black power" only *seems* more concrete than the slogan "Freedom Now" (which the black-power advocates see as soft, vague, hortatory, and inchoate). In fact, the black militants are often captives of the very whites they reject because, by this total rejection, they must do what the whites do *not* do, or vice versa, and they are in the position of other reactive nationalisms, whether in Israel or Ireland

Lacking, as many have pointed out, a territorial base, the advocates of black power are in an even more difficult position than the advocates of other reactive nationalisms. In the absence of a clear program, it will not be easy for them to point to concrete communal organizations as models, either in the economy or on the land. Where there *is* a territorial base, as in some Mississippi counties or in the ghettos, the black-power advocates may discover that by eliminating whites they may succeed in only subjecting themselves to new black despotisms. They may eliminate white policemen from the ghettos only to place themselves under the domination of the most violent Negroes at loose in the ghettos. Black militant students, in combination with college-administration reactionaries, may squeeze white teaching interns out of a Negro college—and yet this may not result in liberation. Many of the upper-class and middle-class Negro students, the cosmopolitans, made extraordinary sacrifices in the early years of the movement, and many could be leaders on their college campuses—because they are intellectually and academically, as well as organizationally, talented. In the present mood, however, the cosmopolitans both wish to and are forced to share mass racial attitudes, at least rhetorically, because the Negro lower class is alleged to be more truly "Negro." Their devotion to the cause of racial solidarity may, for a time, minimize the extent of class conflict within the Negro community, but the cosmopolitans may not always escape being the target of such conflict.

In contrast, the Black Muslim appears to be attempting to transform himself in the process of building a more patriarchal, more hierarchical, more sober, less self-indulgent community. Some of the cosmopolitans are no less sober, but they do not accept the Muslim disciplines; and some who listen to the Muslim slogans, and no more, may gain an all-too-precarious dignity and self-confidence, shored up with invective, a vague sense of allies in the Third World, and a hair style that in some cases can be spectacularly handsome.

Perhaps it is my want of imagination, but I find a community of the dispossessed hard to envisage without charismatic leaders, major organizing drives, and fuller resources. Consider in this connection the interpretations that both locals and cosmopolitans have put on their defeats in Mississippi. They began with the erroneous assumption that if all Negroes were registered to vote, they could somehow be a majority. But they are not, even in Mississippi. And a few local electoral victories scarcely assuage despair. Similarly, the accomplishments—in the face of terrible obstacles—of the Child Development Group of Mississippi (brought about, to be sure, with the support of white churches and a modicum of Federal Government leverage) seem more like total failure than limited success.

In these situations, excessive hopes inevitably lead to extravagant despair. I am reminded of the deep frustration of peasant communities, which—if their momentum is to be kept up—cannot endure a single defeat or even a delay in the course of a string of victories and advances. The disciplined Marxist's willingness to wait for victory is virtually absent; the present need is for "action," at least as occupational therapy. This leads to charisma without an object, to revolutionary tactics without a revolutionary situation, to revolutionary rhetoric that may in turn bring about a new and even deeper cynicism and nihilism.

In an article in *Daedalus* devoted to the Negro in America, James Tobin observes that the balance of payments and de Gaulle's attitude toward it and toward gold may be more important for the Negro American than anything happening autonomously within the Negro community or among its immediate white allies or enemies. A guaranteed annual income, or a negative income tax, might do more to keep Negroes on subsistence farms in the South or in Southern towns, preventing the dispossessed from being forced into the cities or into tent communities, than anything black power can do on its own. No doubt, this is too economistic a view, and leaves aside the immediate question of self-respect vs. powerlessness that is vital for leadership, cohesion, even sanity.

In its integrative aspect, the concept of black power is

helping to reshape Negro self-definitions, whether of beauty or success or outlook, so that (for example) in *Ebony* magazine there are often interesting contradictions between the increasingly militant articles and the still conventional advertising beamed at Negroes upwardly mobile in the white tradition. And where Negroes do live contiguously, they may in the course of time develop— beyond the churches and the lodges and the college fraternities—a growing network of self-help organizations for which concepts of black power (like those of *négritude* in French West Africa) may serve as a partial mystique. Yet it also seems true that no mystique suffices to short-cut the grave problems of economic and cultural development, either in the Third World or here at home, whatever precarious support it provides for the pride of the oppressed.

November 1967